CREATE YOUR OWN
STAGE MAKE-UP
Gill Davies

Back Stage Books
an imprint of Watson-Guptill Publications
New York

First published 2001 by
Back Stage Books,
an imprint of
Watson-Guptill Publications
770 Broadway
New York, NY 10003

www.watsonguptill.com

ISBN 0-8230-7713-6

Published simultaneously in the UK by
A & C Black (Publishers) Limited
Alderman House
37 Soho Square
London W1D 3QZ

ISBN 0-7136-5680-8

CIP catalogue records for this book are
available from the British Library and the
Library of Congress.

While every care has been taken to verify facts
and methods described in this book, neither
the publisher nor the author can accept
liability for any loss, damage or injury,
howsoever caused.

The publishers would be glad to receive
notification of any omissions, errors or
necessary credits in order to
rectify future editions.

Create Your Own Stage Make-up
was conceived, edited and designed by
Playne Books Limited
Chapel House
Trefin, Haverfordwest
Pembrokeshire SA62 5AU
United Kingdom

Author
© Gill Davies 2001

Editor
Vivienne Kay

Research and editorial assistants
Faye Hayes
Linda Lancaster

Photographic manipulation
Rob Key

Designers and illustrators
Richard Cotton
David Playne

Photography by Stewart Royse

Typeset in Glypha

Reproduction by Inka Graphics Limited

Printed in Hong Kong

Contents

5

Contents

Contents

About this book

Make-up is one of the most creative and rewarding aspects of theatre. Taking a fresh look at make-up for stage, *Create Your Own Stage Make-up* aims to help individual make-up artists and performers, groups and schools to explore the exciting world of creating new faces. With its many illustrations and photographs, the step-by-step guidelines and lots of useful lists and charts, this book should prove invaluable to both novice and expert.

The book begins with the basics – from choosing the right materials, preparation and planning, techniques, understanding how to manipulate the effects of light and shade – through to the application of straight make-up.

Specifics follow, such as making up different age groups, various skin types, group make-up, how to use wigs, beards and moustaches, special effects and international roles. Make-up for boys and girls has also been included here.

The last two sections are aimed to stimulate experimentation in order to maximise your make-up skills and to simply have fun finding out just what can be achieved. Special shows and styles are covered, including musicals, melodrama, fantasy, Restoration plays, ballet and dance and then an exciting range of specific characters such as witches, vampires, clowns, birds and pirates.

So, whether the group is a new one trying to put on its first production or an existing society that wants to discover more about this fascinating subject, *Create Your Own Stage Make-up* will be a useful guide to the techniques and a source of new ideas. The make-up team may be a separate entity or it may be that individual actors create their own faces for stage. In either case, we hope this book will provide the know-how and confidence – and the inspiration – to experiment and so develop ever greater skills.

Introduction

As children we learn a great deal about the world in which we live through play, through acting out roles and becoming someone – or something – else. As adults we are less likely to dress up and pretend, unless we happen to happen to be going to a party that requires special costumes; even then the artifice is usually very superficial and, apart from the odd vampire fang, will not necessarily require make-up.

Actors and actresses, on the other hand, spend a good deal of time assuming new characters, helped a good deal by the appropriate make-up. Those who are fortunate enough to belong to a theatre group will soon discover that becoming a different person is fascinating – and can be very enlightening – startling, even!

We tend to take our faces for granted so changing the image you normally see in the mirror for something quite different is a stimulating experiment.

Most women, of course, are used to applying make-up – but usually to make themselves look younger or more glamorous. Deliberately ageing the face, or becoming a ghost, a robot or a cat, is an altogether new venture. It is amazing what skilled stage make-up can achieve.

While *Create Your Own Stage Make-up*, in keeping with the other books in the series, contains many line illustrations, and tables to help the organization aspects of theatre, we have also used photography here. It has been a particularly fascinating experiment to make up just one or two

faces into so many different roles. To see the same young woman's face mutate from its naked beginnings into a plump old woman, a robot, a witch, a 1920s flapper, Cleopatra and a doll has been highly rewarding. Similarly, one young man has been turned into villain, Restoration fop, Toad, and an alien (to mention just a few) while both our victims have been aged, scarred and given a variety of noses, hairstyles, beards and blemishes.

But no book, however well presented and stimulating, is ever the same as the real thing – actually being on stage transformed by make-up into another personality. We hope you have great fun turning the theory into practice!

Gill Davies

Understanding make-up

In early Roman and Greek theatre, and in medieval mystery plays, a character and its dominant features were conveyed by a mask. Today in the Far East, highly colourful and often grotesque masks are used. Usually a mask is an exaggeration of facial features and expression and is a very powerful theatrical device. So much so, that the masks of Tragedy and Comedy remain the symbols of theatre today. The mask remained 'the norm' for centuries: it is still used for Asian performances and in other specialised dramatic performances or mime. Make-up was not widely used in theatre until Elizabethan times.

The first crude powders and paints were made from crushed earth colours and vegetable dyes that had been mixed into animal fats or perfumed oils. In fact, the term 'ham actor' derives from the use by the least affluent actors of ham fat from a piece of rind, as a make-up base. Another colorant such as brick dust was then applied over the top of this thick grease base.

As cinema techniques advanced, improved cosmetics were created

Make-up became just a little more refined once women were allowed to take to the stage in Restoration times. None the less, there was still a heavy base – made of white fat and white lead. White chalk was applied over this, burnt cork defined the eyes and brows, while red carmine added emphasis to the lips and cheeks.

The impoverished 'ham' actor used ham fat as a base

Make-up began to be produced commercially during the nineteenth century but stage make-up still remained somewhat mask-like through the gas lighting period and the first arrival of electricity. Even the movies and close-up photography did not change the style of cosmetics as the cinema's powerful carbon lights required make-up to be just as heavy.

This all changed with the 'talkies'. The sizzling carbon lights were too noisy once sound was part of the recording and were replaced by huge, silent, incandescent electric light bulbs. Panochromatic film arrived at much the same time and this, together with the new lighting, exposed the harshness of the existing make-up.

Different materials were needed and Max Factor created a new range of much finer cosmetics. Before long these were being implemented for theatre work as well. Actors appreciated the more comfortable feel of the make-up and the greater finesse made possible.

Understanding why make-up is needed

Understanding why make-up is needed

Make-up is needed to make the actor's face look right for the character from the audience viewpoint. The actor's face is one of the most dominant factors on the stage. In historic times, masks entirely hid the actor's face and simply substituted them with another. The expression was fixed and changing emotion could be conveyed only by gesture and the body stance.

Today's stage make-up, on the other hand, is 'malleable'. If well executed, it becomes part of the role creation without in any way inhibiting or cloaking facial expressions. The manifestation of emotion, however subtle, can be given greater impetus. Even those members of the audience who are at the greatest distance and so cannot readily detect that raised eyebrow or a minute lift of the chin, will still be aware how the actor is using the full complement of natural reactions to build the overall feel of the character. This enhanced role portrayal, underscored by appropriate make-up, will certainly be appreciated by everyone – not least the actors and actresses themselves; they welcome costume and make-up as part of the kit that helps them step into another character.

There are on occasions, of course, those make-ups that are extreme and may involve three-dimensional additions and rebuilding the face to such an extent that the actor's freedom of expression does becomes somewhat limited. This might apply to a heavy animal or monster make-up or to a very extensive ageing operation. But even these complete rebuilding make-ups remain individual and part of the actor's actual face. However extensive, this is still make-up, not a fixed mask.

Objectives

Make-up serves several important purposes. Briefly it helps to:

Define characters

Stage characters need to have an instant impact on the audience. Their roles must be complemented by the make-up. A whole range of age-groups and degrees of glamour or ugliness, nationality, state of health, and types of personality can be conveyed to the audience by the right make-up.

Instil confidence in the cast

Just as costumes help the actors to feel their way into the role, so make-up too helps the actor to establish his or her character. Make-up can help actors to simply look better or younger – or to become quite different people from their everyday selves. If the actors are comfortable with the make-up, and excited by the changes they see in the mirror, it will help enormously to boost their self-confidence.

Counteract the draining effect of the lighting

Over the years, styles of make-up have changed and, in general, this has been because of technical changes, the way the lighting has altered, rather than merely the following of fashion – although this has had its effect of course. The extreme, white Restoration make-up, for example, was in the same style as that exhibited by the fashion-conscious of the day, male and female! As actors moved from open-air performances in daylight to candlelit theatre, then gaslight, electric light, limelight and the cinema studio, so the make-up has mutated to meet the effects of the particular light source.

Strong stage lighting makes skin colour paler and can flatten the features so a major purpose of the make-up is to counteract this effect. It is therefore important to establish what lighting will be used when, in which colours and just how powerful it is going to be. The make-up cannot be isolated from these effects.

Understanding faces

Bone structure

In everyday life it is easy to forget that we are all of us skeletons, albeit cloaked in muscles, flesh, skin and, finally, clothes. However, to understand faces and how to use make-up to best effect, it is essential to be aware of the bone structure of the skull. Apart from anything else, if the character is supposed to be very old, ill or starving, the bones will need to be emphasised – so it is important to know where they are. But even with conventional make-up for a young, healthy person, the bone structure is a vital element upon which to build shape and dimension. Just as Michelangelo studied anatomy in order to be able to represent the entire human body properly through his art, so the skull is the underlying framework of a face and deserves some appreciation by the make-up artist.

There are many hollows and prominences. It can be a useful exercise to stand in front of a mirror in a good light and to see if you can trace these with your fingertips. Begin to map out the contours of your face. If friends or rela-

Understanding faces

Bone structure front view and profile

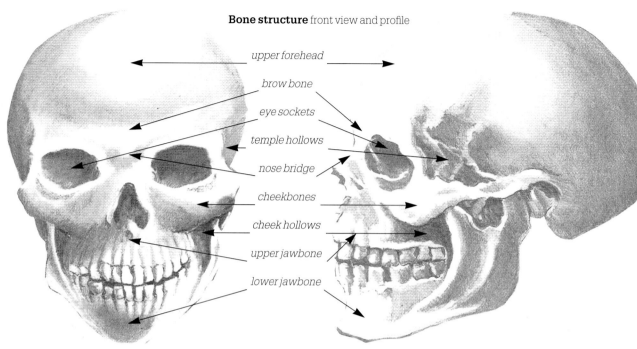

upper forehead

brow bone

eye sockets

temple hollows

nose bridge

cheekbones

cheek hollows

upper jawbone

lower jawbone

tives are willing, feel their faces and heads too; see if you can identify in which ways these are different to your own skull.

If actors or actresses are likely to be applying their own make-up, it is

especially useful to be familiar with each feature. Cheekbones and cheek hollows are particularly important as these are vital areas that will be highlighted and shadowed when altering a face with make-up.

Although human skulls seem very similar at a glance, there are, in fact, many individual characteristics to be discovered. This is what enables artists assisting historians or the police to construct 'identikit' images or models of faces from a skull – and explains why blind people can 'feel' a face and identify individuals.

Face shapes

Faces can be measured in equal thirds across for width and equal thirds down for length. If the balance is incorrect for the required effect, this can be altered by make-up and hair (see page 53). Face shapes can be defined most simply according to the

seven categories described below.

Oval
Usually seen as the ideal balance

Round
Full cheeks and a full jawline

Square
Short face with a wide forehead and square jawline

Oblong
A long, narrow face

Triangle
A wide jawline and narrow cheekbones

Inverted triangle
A wide forehead, wide-set eyes and high cheekbones

Diamond
A narrow forehead, high strong cheekbones and a receding chin.

Try to trace the following with your fingertips:

upper forehead

brow bone

eye sockets

temple hollows

nose bridge

cheekbones

cheek hollows

upper jawbone

lower jawbone

Features

Features

The face is a composite blend of individual features. Every feature can be used to give the right emphasis to a character. Each single element can be highlighted or altered by make-up and, in certain cases (like false noses), entirely new ones may be created for a make-up! Whether the role is a kind old lady, a murderous villain or a feline in the musical *Cats*, the features must be analysed and decisions taken as to how to make them up to best effect.

Eyes

Of all the facial features, the eyes are the most important. Not only do they reveal a great deal about the character and emotions, but they are relatively easy to change with make-up. Every woman applying her own 'domestic' make-up will agree that making up the eyes is usually the most vital and protracted part of the exercise; this applies to normal stage make-up too.

Character by type of eye

Normal eyes
Normal Caucasian eyes are not too deeply set and are almond shaped. They are set one eye width apart. Upper and lower lids just 'clip' across the tip and bottom of the iris circle. The brows arch gently.

Analytical eyes, suggesting thinkers and authors
The eyes are deep set, under straight lowered brows.

Dishonest, sullen or moody characters
These can be suggested by deep set eyes that are too close together, with heavy brows.

A sinister character
Small eyes should narrow obliquely while the eyebrows wing up from the root of the nose.

A happy, kind person
The eyes should be slightly narrowed with laughter lines that lift upwards at the outer corners.

Dreamers and poets
Make the eyes look prominent, with heavy lids to suggest an aesthetic nature.

Silly or susceptible, innocent characters
Wide eyes should be prominent and set too far apart, with raised brows.

Sorrowful or stressed characters
The eyes should be downward-sloping with eyebrows that lift in the centre.

Eyebrows

Just changing the eyebrows alone can convey quite dramatically different effects.

Here, in each case, the eye shapes remain the same but the eyebrows have been altered.

Thoughtful and serious

Happy, content

Surprise and uncertainty

Kind and sympathetic

Quizzical

Solidity, certainty, determination

Concentration

Amazement

Features

In control

Strong, powerful

Unsure, hesitant

Waiting, patient

Confident

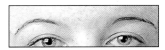

Refined, perhaps a little shy

Strange, devilish

Mouths

Mouths are almost as expressive as eyes. They are in constant motion as they are used to convey all sorts of feelings, emotions and temperament. Mouths can be reshaped by using overpainting and highlighting but should never be 'overdone' so as to dominate the eyes. Very careful treatment is needed when making up men's mouths as they should not look as if they are wearing lipstick – unless this is intended!

Obviously the area and the muscles around the mouth are important too. For example, in an ageing make-up this is an area of fine wrinkles.

Examples of character types suggested by mouth shapes:

Normal mouth: female
The classic female mouth has fairly full lips with a cupid's bow on the upper lip.

Normal mouth: male
The classic male mouth is less full and the upper lip is not so obviously bow-shaped.

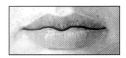

Sensual characters
Sensuality is suggested by large mouths with full lips.

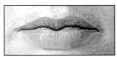

A moody selfish character
This can be suggested by a mouth having downward-drooping corners and a full lower lip.

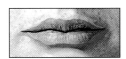

A scheming, malicious character
The mouth should be wide with curving lips.

A strong, determined person, who is likely to be wicked
Create a mouth that is straight and tightly-closed with thin lips.

A strong, determined person, who is good
Create a protruding lower lip that is raised over the top lip.

Weariness and sorrow
Use downward-drooping corners with thin lower lips.

A disdainful character
Create a protruding upper lip that projects over the lower lip.

Selfish vindictive characters
They should have a small tight mouth.

Noses

Noses come in a surprising variety of shapes which can vary in breadth, symmetry and nostril shape from the front-on view as well as in profile. Only the bottom section is flexible and so noses convey type, character and race rather than any immediate emotional reactions. They are very easy to remodel with nose putty and can change appearances quite dramatically. Complete false noses are also available for, say, an evil witch's long, hooked nose. There are Grecian and Augustinian noses, Roman noses, snub noses and many a variation in between these.

Grecian nose

Augustinian nose

Roman nose

Snub nose
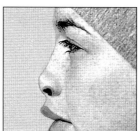

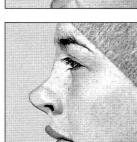

Examples of characters suggested by various nose shapes

A strong, vital, determined person
This is conveyed by a short straight nose or a Roman nose hooked in the middle or top. If the Roman nose is hooked at the tip instead, this determination might lead to treachery or malice.

A mischievous character
A snub nose with the depression at the tip

Immaturity
A snub nose with the depression at the middle

Nobility
A long straight Grecian or Augustinian nose is supposed to be the classic indication of noble birth and sensitivity.

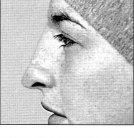

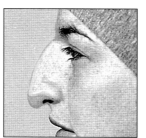

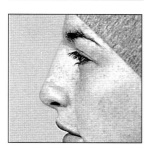

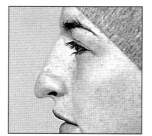

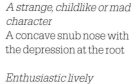

A strange, childlike or mad character
A concave snub nose with the depression at the root

Enthusiastic lively characters
A short, straight nose tipped up at the end

A determined character
A long, straight nose with a depressed tip

A melancholy character
A long, straight nose with a depressed tip – best combined with eyes that droop downwards

Other factors

Ears

Ears are fairly standard shapes although some stick out more than others! The only characters that need special ears are fairy folk, animals, aliens, comics and someone who has been in a fight and therefore needs a cauliflower ear.

Hands and neck

Hands are very important. If the skin colour is to change or the character to be aged, this effect will be totally undermined if the hands are not made up to co-ordinate appropriately. And no witch's or mandarin's make-up is complete without long fingernails.

Most actors gesticulate; many use their hands all the time. Always consider the potential of the hands and how much they can contribute to the make-up.

In the same way, the make-up should not stop short at the chin. The neck must be made up as well or the make-up will look like a mask.

Other factors

Reading, research and observation will help the make-up artist to build up know-how on all these sorts of factors. Watch the faces of all those around you.

Become aware of feature and expression. It can be useful, too, to keep a file with notes, magazine clippings or whatever, for future reference.

Meanwhile, a greater understanding of faces and how much they work and change will be the best possible foundation for the application of the very best make-up!

Age

Understanding the ageing process is vital for the make-up artist. Whether adding years or taking them away, the following features of the effects of age will need to be created, diminished or removed:

1
Muscles lose their firmness and begin to sag.

2
Depending on the person's weight, flesh may fall into folds or sink in.

3
Wrinkles appear, especially on the brows, around the eyes and mouth, on the neck and hands

4
The bone structure becomes more apparent.

5
Skin colour loses its youthful bloom.

6
Necks become scrawny

7
Hair thins and turns grey or white; it may recede or fall out.

8
Men's eyebrows become coarse and bushy; women's may fall out.

9
In advanced old age:
. . . the gums shrivel and teeth may drop out,
. . . complexions become very pale,
. . . lips may be bluish, and eyelids pink.

The section on pages 62-68 explains how to achieve these ageing effects.

More considerations on make-up

Of course, over and above these most obvious considerations of face, feature and age, there are always special factors to take into account with every play and every role.

Each well-planned and carefully executed make-up is the result of multiple detailing and the following factors may also need to be taken into account:

1
Ethnic groups

2
Hereditary factors – are two or more characters related?

3
Health

4
Temperament

5
The type of production and overall approach (is it straight, comic, stylised?)

6
Time and place (is it a play set in history or in, say, a hot climate?)

Understanding colour

It is not necessary for the make-up artist to be a physics expert but some knowledge of the science of colour and how this works – both in pigment and in light – will be very useful. Colour can play some surprising tricks on the uninitiated, so if the artist

Understanding colour

Colour cone *Colours vary in intensity. Some are more brilliant than others and these move further from the centre of the wheel as they intensify. A paint or make-up can be made paler by adding white (it is then called a tint) or darker by adding black (and is then called a shade)*

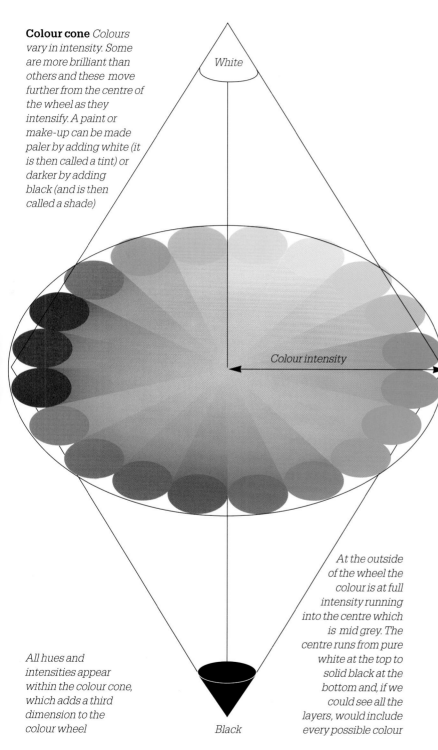

White

Colour intensity

All hues and intensities appear within the colour cone, which adds a third dimension to the colour wheel

Black

At the outside of the wheel the colour is at full intensity running into the centre which is mid grey. The centre runs from pure white at the top to solid black at the bottom and, if we could see all the layers, would include every possible colour

Composite colours *Many lighting effects are made by using filters in front of the lights. Check if these change the colour of the make-up on stage*

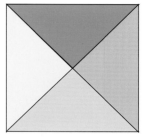

Four-colour composite

Four-colour composite

Two-colour composite

Two-colour composite

Understanding colour

wants to achieve the intended results, and not to make any errors through ignorance, some understanding of colour theory is essential. For example, different coloured lights can change the colour of make-up and a strong violet eye shadow will turn almost black when lit by a yellow or green light.

Colour mixing

Given the three primary colours, you can mix any colour you wish. Furthermore, given white and black, you can then mix any tint or shade of that colour.

Generally it is not necessary to mix your own colours with cosmetics since the manufacturers provide such a wide range, but once you understand the principles of mixing, you can adjust a colour by adding either, black, white or another colour – and when you are applying one colour on top of another, there may be occasions when you wish to blend them together.

Colour in light

Lighting plays an important part in stage make-up effects, so it is vital to understand the difference between the primary colours in pigment (red, blue and yellow) and the primary colours in light (red, blue and green). If you mix the light primary colours together with equal intensity, they will produce white light.

In the theatre, coloured filters (or gelatines) are placed in front of incandescent lights to produce a range of different colour tints and shades. These colour filters will absorb all the colours in the spectrum except their own. For example, a blue filter will allow only blue light to pass through on to the stage.

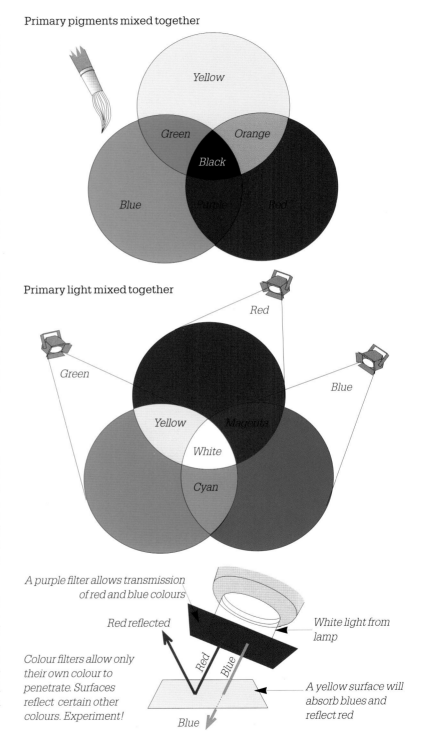

Primary pigments mixed together

Yellow

Green

Orange

Black

Blue

Purple

Red

Primary light mixed together

Red

Green

Blue

Yellow

Magenta

White

Cyan

A purple filter allows transmission of red and blue colours

Red reflected

Red

Blue

White light from lamp

Colour filters allow only their own colour to penetrate. Surfaces reflect certain other colours. Experiment!

A yellow surface will absorb blues and reflect red

Blue

18

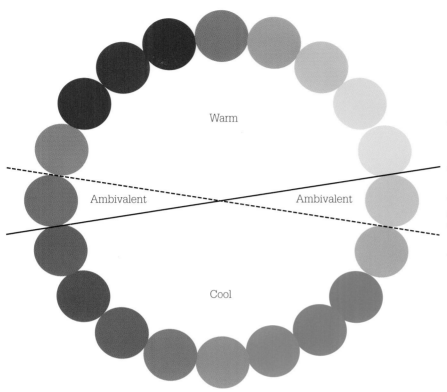

Warm

Ambivalent

Ambivalent

Cool

Warm and cool colours

Warm colours are on the top half of the wheel and cool colours on the bottom half of the wheel. The ambivalent colours (yellow-green and lavender) can appear either warm or cool, depending upon which contrasting colour is set against them

How make-up colours change under the lights

Make-up→ Lights↓	Red	Orange	Yellow	Green	Blue	Violet
Red	Fades and disappears	Becomes lighter	Becomes white	Becomes much darker	Becomes dark grey	Goes black
Yellow	Remains red	Fades slightly	Fades and disappears	Becomes dark grey	Becomes dark grey	Becomes nearly black
Green	Becomes much darker	Darkens	Darkens	Becomes very pale green	Turns dark green	Becomes nearly black
Blue	Darkens	Becomes much darker	Turns light mauve	Lightens	Turns pale blue	Turns light mauve
Violet	Becomes pale red	Lightens	Turns pink	Becomes pale blue	Darkens	Becomes very pale
Neutral colours – black, brown and grey – remain almost the same under different lights, apart from a small change in tonal value.						

Understanding colour

Primary light falling
on primary pigment
in costumes or make-
up is yet another mix

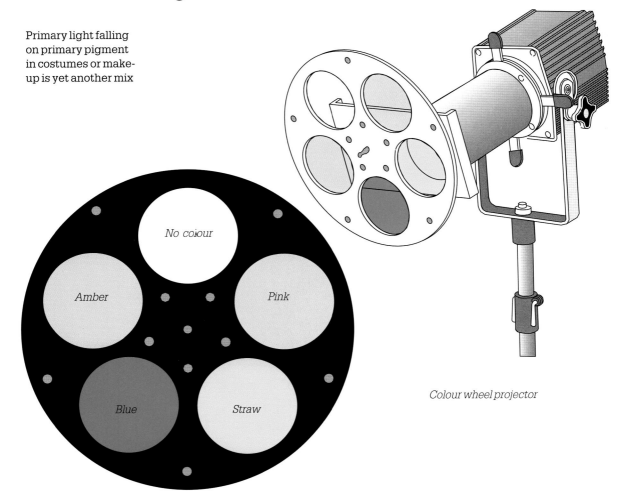

Colour wheel projector

There are over seventy filters or 'gels' to choose from. The most common lighting colours are flesh (pale pink), surprise pink (cold neutral), daylight blue, steel blue, straw, gold and bastard amber (warm neutral).

Normal stage lighting generally contains a combination of cold and warm neutral lights – made up from ambers, straws, golds and surprise pink.

This neutral mixture, combined with the colour of incandescent bulbs, tends to be yellow in tone, so that make-up should be slightly on the pink or warm side in order to appear as natural as possible under balanced stage lighting.

> Under normal, slightly yellow stage lighting, make-up should be slightly on the pink or warm side

Pigment colours in light

The chart on page 19 gives an indication of how coloured lights will alter different colours of pigment. It shows only the impact of strong coloured light on brilliant hues. It does not take into account any subtleties of make-up colours and stage lighting but does give an indication of how coloured filters will affect different make-ups.

Flesh pink will make only a small change to most make-ups and is, generally speaking, one of the most flattering stage lights.

Very strong red light will be disastrous to any make-up; skin tone will almost disappear, average rouging will totally fade away and dark reds become brown. However, since a strong red light is used only for very dramatic

Understanding light and shade

effects, the audience will expect the make-up to look strange.

Amber and orange filters will also ruin a good make-up. Skin tones will become yellowed and shading details look dirty. This light should be used only to light the set. Bastard amber, on the other hand, is an extremely flattering light. It tends to intensify the pinks and flesh tones and adds life and sparkle to a make-up.

Green light greys all skin tones and rouges and gives a macabre effect, but since this is generally being used in an eerie situation, the audience will accept the effect quite willingly.

Blue light will give a sickly grey tone to the skin and will darken lip and cheek colouring but since it is mostly used for moonlight effects, this is acceptable. However, if a long love scene is to be played in moonlight, this colour can be disturbing, so it will help in these circumstances if some supplementary warm light can be played on the actors' faces.

Straw and gold filters have very little effect on the make-up, except perhaps to warm it slightly. Violet light tends to intensify the reds, so play down the rouge and avoid pink skin tones which will become florid.

The biggest problem is that lighting can change very rapidly during the course of a play and obviously it is not possible to change the make-up at the same rate. It is a good idea to make a careful check of your make-up during lighting rehearsals and try to modify it to suit the main lighting changes. If, however, you find you are unable to do this and the lighting is really spoiling the make-up, then a word in the director's ear is necessary, so that some lighting adjustments can be made.

Understanding light and shade

Light falling on an object creates highlights and shadows, so defining the shape. This effect can be created with make-up so as to give the illusion of a three-dimensional object where none, in fact, exists. Thus the wrinkles and folds of old age, an injury, swelling, hollow cheeks, a broken nose and so on can be imitated and look far more real than would be possible with any flat crayon effect.

Light can create either a soft or a hard-edged shadow. In the first case, the divisions between the dark and light areas are sharp and immediate. This usually occurs where the object has flat, hard angles.

In the second, the change from dark to light is less obvious; it is soft and gradual. This occurs where the planes of the object are curved or rounded.

So . . . sharp edges and corners create strong lights and darks. Curved surfaces result in an infinite number of intermediate shades between these two extremes.

Of course, the position of the light source will make a difference as to where the shadows lie but, whatever the direction of the light and whatever the shape of the object, light will highlight the part of the object upon which it falls and leave a lowlight on the opposite side.

Fine artists use a combination of both hard and soft-edged shadows in drawing and painting to mimic this and so achieve a natural effect. In the same way, a make-up artist will use both kinds of shadow effects in whatever way best imitates the natural play of light upon face and feature.

Perspective

There are also the effects of perspective to be considered. At a greater distance (for example, when looking at tall buildings or at far-way mountains) the further away from the viewer, the greyer the objects appear as the distinction between black and white becomes less and less defined. This may be a useful thing to imitate when trying to make some features more prominent or to recede more than others. For example, furrows in the brow are not all at identical levels and can seem more natural if some are given sharper definition than others.

A hard-edged shadow   *A soft-edged shadow*

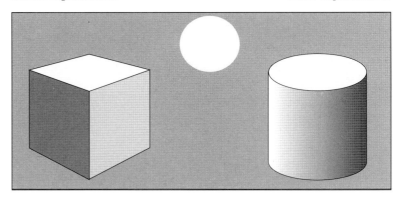

21

Understanding light and shade

Practise the effects

It can be useful to practise drawing shadows with soft pencils or charcoal to discover for yourself the effects of hard and soft edges and what degrees of blending work best. Try drawing a hard-edged box and a cylinder to examine what happens with sharp, hard edges and then soft, rounded edges. After this, it might, perhaps, be a worthwhile exercise to try drawing the folds of a drape or curtain – which are not too dissimilar to the folds that occur in flesh.

Once these techniques have been grasped, it is time to see if you can achieve the same effects with make-up on the face.

It is worth practising one or two make-up effects that will demon-strate the principles of light and shade especially well. With these tech-niques perfected, the make-up artist will be armed with one of the most important tools he or she will ever need. Using light and shade will be the basis of nearly every make-up effect – and fundamentally important when ageing characters.

Nasolabial folds

The nasolabial folds are the lines that run down from the nostril to the cor-ners of the mouth. These folds gradually become etched much deeper as you age.

Creating these folds is a good exam-ple of how to use a combination of both soft and hard-edged shadows and highlights so as to create a natural ageing effect.

1 Using a square-ended brush, draw a line of shadow along the centre crease of the nasolabial fold.

2 With a clean brush, carefully blend the top edge of the line upwards onto the cheek.

3 Apply highlight below the shadow and blend along the lip but make sure that you leave a hard edge of highlight against the dark crease.

4 Now apply a line of highlight along the top of the fold and blend this gently onto the cheek.

This kind of ageing, using light and shadow, can be repeated with many other make-up effects – such as the lines on the forehead, folds on the jaw-line and veins on the hands.

Hollow cheeks

A realistic effect of hollow cheeks is created with soft, blended shadows and highlight.

1 Suck in cheeks. Make a Y in a dark, shading colour with a 6-9mm (0.25-0.6ins) brush.

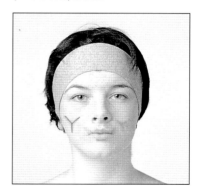

2 Blend away the outside edges of shadow until it looks like a soft hol-low. The top edge should be only slightly softened while the bottom edges should be faded out almost completely.

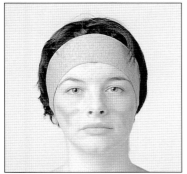

3 Now add a strong band of highlight along the cheekbone.

4 Blend away the top edge of the highlight so that it merges into the foundation.

All the backstage team must understand each other's needs and work well together to achieve the best results

5 Blend the lower edge of the highlight into the shadow.

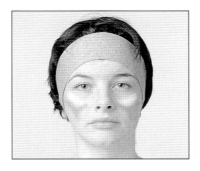

Summing up

Make-up has the potential to be an intricate, highly skilled art form. It can be used by the individual actor or by make-up artists to achieve many different levels of effect.

Depending upon the size of the stage and venue, the levels and colours of the lighting, and the demands of the various roles, the approach can be

fairly relaxed and simple or become a major factor in the production, requiring a professional attitude and a good deal of time prior to curtain-up.

In many cases, as societies grow and develop, so the attitude to the make-up and the standards demanded will grow in relationship to this.

However, whatever the status of the group – whether it is new and learning, established and growing or whether it is a highly professional society – a thorough understanding of faces, colour and light; and why make-up is such a useful tool – will be a great asset.

Armed with this information and know-how, the make-up team will be able to make a better assessment of what each production involves and have a clearer vision of aims, potential problems and priorities as they begin the organising process.

Organisation

Like any other aspect of theatre production, good make-up requires good planning. Everything needs to be thought through and organised well in advance. The play should be studied, characters discussed with the director and individual actors, while a plan of campaign is devised for the performances. Meanwhile the equipment and stock must be checked through and sorted. Even if individual actors and actresses provide their own make-up – as often happens – there should be someone responsible for making sure in good time that everyone has everything they need.

As a general guide to duties, the make-up department needs to:

1 Take care of the make-up kit and keep it well stocked, purchasing new items as needed.

2 Keep and update a stocklist.

3 Create a 'faces file' that acts as a portrait gallery of the make-up done for the group. Include both the rough sketches and the photographs of finished effects. This will be very useful for future reference. It can be helpful to add to this photographs of other inspiring ideas you come across – as a source for future productions.

4 Plan the make-up for each production carefully.

5 Make sure a good team of helpers is always available to undertake the make-up for the show. Work out a rota if necessary.

6 During performances, organise the dressing room or make-up room. Lay out all the make-up so that it will be ready in good time for each performance.

7 Tidy everything away afterwards and note any replacement make-up needed.

Equipment and materials

Many groups will launch their first play with a relatively small make-up kit. Much depends on the style of the show. If this is a musical or revue with lots of performers and several fantasy characters then a good stock of make-up will be essential. A straight play with a small cast, on the other hand, needs a relatively basic set of make-up supplies unless there are a number of characters that need to be aged.

If starting from scratch, ask the actresses and back-stage members if they have any left-over cosmetics that they do not need. They may have some lipsticks with colours that do not suit them or foundations that turned out to be too dark. Any such contributions can be useful additions. The more specialised items, such as stage blood, will gradually be accumulated as the need arises.

Many make-up kits are launched with just a few basic stocks of foundation, powder and cleansing cream, augmented by the cast's own make-up and left-overs that can be begged from various sources.

This initial stock will gradually be added to and replaced over the years.

Basic make-up kit

If the budget will allow, a good basic kit will include the following:

Basic make-up kit

Boxes with dividers to keep everything tidy – tool kits and fishing boxes are ideal

A selection of brushes, from fine eye-liner tips and lip brushes to plump rouge mops

Make-up remover and tissues

Cotton (wool) balls and cotton buds (swabs)

Powder puffs

Foundations in various shades: these can be greasepaint, stick, cake or liquid bases

Sticks or pots of lining colours for adding detail

Rouge

Translucent face powder

Lipsticks in a good range of shades

Eye shadow in a variety of colours

Mascara – to include black, brown, and navy

Eyebrow pencils

Eyeliners – pencil, cake and liquid

False eyelashes

Scissors

Hair bands, grips and pins

Towels

Robes to protect clothing

Skin tonic for using on oily skins before make-up

Water

Basic make-up kit

Cosmetic boxes

Clear plastic boxes are excellent because it is easy to see what is inside. Plastic tool or fishing-tackle boxes, with cantilevered trays, are also ideal. They come in different sizes, with a variable number of trays.

Brushes, sponges and powder puffs

Brushes
A selection of brushes in various sizes will be needed, from fine eye-liner tips for eye make-up and fine detail to the plumpest rouge mop. Good quality sable ones are best for fine work.

Powder puffs
The flat velour type is best. They need to be washed frequently so buy at least two.

Make-up bases or foundation

Hard greasepaint
One of the first commercial stage make-ups, greasepaint comes in stick form. The colours are limited and usually you need to blend two or more sticks together to achieve the right skin tone. However, many different skin colours can be created with a relatively small number of sticks, and hard greasepaint is inexpensive so it is particularly good for those on a tight budget. It can give an old-fashioned masklike result and so must be used with great care.

Soft greasepaint
This soft, creamy-textured paint is much quicker and easier to apply than

> **Cosmetic sponges**
>
> These are used for the application of foundation and body makeup:
>
> Fine plastic foam sponges are good for cake, cream and grease foundations.
>
> If they are of a very fine texture with no large holes, natural sponges are excellent for cake make-ups.
>
> Foam-rubber sponges can be used for cream and grease foundations but sometimes disintegrate quite quickly.

hard greasepaint but tends to be very shiny unless extremely well blended and generously powdered. Some

> **Brushes needed**
>
> A face-powder brush is useful for removing excess powder.
>
> **1**
> 3mm (0.125 inch) flat for eye lining and fine character detail
>
> **2**
> 6mm (0.25 inch) flat for blending eyeshadow and character highlights and shadows
>
> **3**
> 9mm (0.375 inch) flat for blending large areas of light and shade
>
> **4**
> Number 2 filbert, for eye lining and fine character detail
>
> **5**
> Number 6 filbert for application of lip colour, eyeshadow and character light and shade
>
> **6**
> Rouge mop for application of dry rouge colours

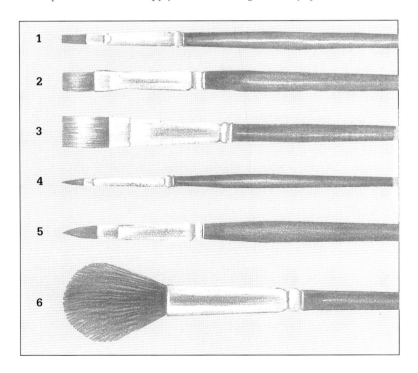

Basic make-up kit

manufacturers produce it in a limited range of colours that need blending in the same way as hard greases; others produce ranges of ready-blended colours which are rather more convenient to apply.

Cream-stick make-ups

These make-up bases, first created for film and television make-up, are now widely used and are available in a large range of colours. Formulated on a non-greasy cream base, they are easy to apply, comfortable to wear and, when thoroughly powdered, they are long lasting. However, they are considerably more expensive than greasepaint.

Liquid make-ups

Liquid-based make-ups are mainly used for body make-up and are produced in the same colours as greasepaint. There are a number of liquid bases in day make-up ranges, but these are not strong enough to use on large stages with bright lighting.

Cake make-up

This is a greaseless, water-soluble foundation that is applied with a wet sponge. Many actors prefer cake make-up to greasepaint because of its easy application and removal. It is non-greasy and creates less perspiration than greasepaint – so is extremely popular with dancers and any performers who perspire freely. Cake make-ups dry very quickly and are difficult to mix or use for detail so they tend to be applied for basic, straight work and for body make-up. They are extremely useful for quick-change make-ups and for certain racial effects.

Although relatively expensive, cake make-ups do not need to be powdered, and this balances the cost to some extent.

Sticks or pots of lining colours

These colours are used to add detail to the make-up. They come as hard and soft greasepaint. Hard greasepaint liners are supplied in a very slim stick form. Soft grease liners are supplied in small tins or pots. Both are available in a wide range of colours, including grey, brown, maroon, blue, green, black and white. There is also a range of reds available in both textures but these are usually referred to as lip colours.

Lipsticks

These are not essential if you have a wide enough range of the lining colours. However, you are almost bound to aquire them by default! Sort them into colours. Some might be useful as rouge under the final powder. A pot of lip gloss can also be useful for some glamorous make-ups.

Rouge

Cake or dry powder rouge is used to touch up a completed make-up using a rouge mop or in conjunction with a cake make-up by using a moist sponge. The least expensive, basic colours are the most useful.

Face powder

One good translucent powder is all that is necessary. This can be used over all colours of foundation, from very pale to black, without seriously distorting the colour.

Eye make-up

There is no longer any need to buy special stage eye make-up, no matter what effect is required.

Eyeshadow

Apart from the basic grease lining colours, eyeshadow can be a powder, cream, creaseless liquid or pencil in a variety of colours – all of which can be used to good effect in the theatre.

Mascara

Black, brown, navy and more exotic colours are available. There are varieties that are waterproof, some that are good for sensitive eyes and those who wear contact lenses, and some that add fibres to lengthen the eyelashes while others are supposed to make the lashes curl!

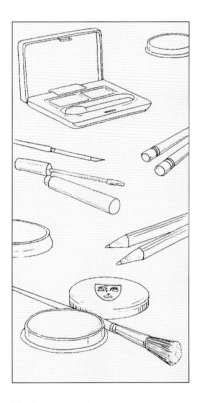

Eyebrow pencils

Black and dark brown are the only colours that are absolutely necessary. Any good, wooden eyebrow pencil is satisfactory, but professional pencils are usually longer and will be more economical.

Supplies, storage and stock checks

Eyeliners

Apart from pencils and greasepaint lining colours, there are water-soluble cake liners and liquid liners. Cake liners are the most versatile since they can be used to achieve sharp clear lines or blended away to a soft shadowy line. Liquid liner is usually packaged with an automatic wand applicator; it is much more difficult to blend away but will achieve a good, clearly defined line.

False eyelashes

False eyelashes can be very effective on stage. Care must be taken to choose lashes that are heavy enough to register well from a distance but not so dense that they cast shadows over the eye.

Make-up removing

It is important to remove make-up properly, especially for those with sensitive skins. Your kit should include cold cream, baby oil or some such remover, as well as cleansing tissues and cotton wool balls to wipe away the make-up.

Cotton buds (swabs) will also remove smudged mascara and correct mistakes. Use eye make-up remover pads for the most delicate areas and plenty of clean water and towels.

Both cream and liquid removers are equally efficient. Water-soluble cream removers leave the skin feeling refreshed but are usually a little more expensive. Baby oils are good but a cosmetically balanced cleanser is better. Skin tonic may help to remove any final traces of grease, make-up or remover after cleansing the face. People with skin problems should take great care with their cleansing routine and always use an antibacterial type of remover.

Extras

The basic kit will need to be added to as the specific demands of each production are met. In due course they will undoubtedly be needed.

Extras needed

Latex and Derma Wax for special effects such as scars and warts

False fingernails (useful for witches and Eastern potentates)

False noses of various shapes and sizes

Nose putty

Spirit gum

Black tooth enamel – always use proper black tooth enamel. Anything else will not adhere properly to the surface of a tooth and will wash or rub off.

Clown white

Sparkle in gel

Stage blood

Wigs, hairpieces and hair

The make-up person or costume department will generally be responsible for hairstyles and may need to organise the hire or purchase of wigs, and to dress these if necessary – as well as helping with actors' own hair styling. Whether or not the make-up person can actually style hair or not varies from one theatre group to another. The make-up person may act merely in an advisory capacity but it is a great bonus if he or she can organise professional help or actually style hair appropriately (see also pages 76-79).

Beards and moustaches

Crepe will be needed for false beards, moustaches, eyebrows and stubble. These pieces can be bought ready-made but making your own always gives a far more convincing result (see pages 80-84).

Supplies, storage and stock checks

Always keep a clear list of what make-up is in stock and update this regularly. The make-up kit will probably need 'topping up' after each production. In some instances, replacements may be needed during the run of a show – always keep an eye open for anything that is running low. Then, when you are tidying up after a play, make a note of what has been used and should be replaced. A further stock check will be needed as soon as the next play is cast and you have analysed its specific requirements.

There are many suppliers of stage make-up and some of these are listed on page 152. However, many items such as lipsticks and eye make-up do not need to come from specialist suppliers and can be bought from any store selling cosmetics. Keep an eye open for bargains and sales stock.

NEED   EYEBROW PENCILS 2+
BLUE EYELINER
TRANSLUCENT POWDER
SCARLET LIPSTICK
NEW LIP BRUSH
COLD CREAM
PAPER TOWEL
PAPER TISSUES - 6 BOXES

Choosing make-up colours

The make-up should be kept somewhere cool – there is nothing worse than melted lipstick – and relatively accessible so that stock checks are easy. Often the make-up artist will keep his or her own kit at home but if the society owns and pays for the stock, it should, ideally, be under the society's control, somewhere safe but on common ground!

Choosing make-up colours

Manufacturers often discontinue colours without warning and are continually introducing new ones, so specific make-up shades cannot be recommended. In any case, choosing colours is very personal. They look different on every skin and it is important that each make-up should be individual, not a stereotyped copy. When choosing make-up, you must rely on your own judgement and the advice of your supplier.

Lip and rouge colours

Lip and rouge colours are divided into the following four groups:

1
Light-red group: clear light-reds with no blue undertones

2
Medium-red group: strong, light blue-reds

3
Dark-red group; dark-blue reds

4
Lake group; dark-brown reds

Skin colours and bases

The fifteen skin colours listed here are the actual skin tones of the flesh and also the kinds of colours that you will need to be able to create with foundation bases. This is only a guide but when analysing the tone of the actor's skin – and the colour that the role requires – some greater definition may be needed. When analysing a specific character, do augment these categories with more detail as needed.

1
Pale group: pale flesh colours that are neither strongly pink nor beige

2
Ivory group: very pale ivory colours

3
Creamy group: medium-beige colours

4
Pink group: very strong, pink flesh tones

5
Peach group: clear, warm-medium skin tones

6
Florid group: strong, deep-red skin tones

7
Light-tan group: light-tan skin tones

8
Deep-tan group: strong tans

9
Warm-tan group: very deep warm tans

10
Olive group: Mediterranean and Latin skin tones

11
Olive-brown group: Asiatic skin tones

12
Dark-brown group: Afro-Caribbean colours

13
Sallow group: yellow-grey skin tones

14
Yellow group: Asian skin tones

15
Drab group: yellow-grey browns

Plan of campaign

1 Read play

2 Analyse appearance of characters

3 Discuss overall style and aims of production and the essence of individual characters with both the producer and the actors concerned.

4 Research any necessary background information and how to achieve effects.

5 Make plot of timing, noting any fast changes or when large numbers of people will need help with their make-up at once.

6 Draw rough sketches of make-up for any special characters.

7 Attend rehearsals to check out appropriateness of ideas and incorporate any changes or additions that occur.

8 Check through stock and buy any new make-up required.

9 Organise hire of wigs.

10 Organise any extra help needed and plan who is doing what when.

11 Supervise make-up and hair styling at dress rehearsals. Allow ample opportunity to practise any specially difficult or previously untried types of make-up.

12 Check effect out front and make any necessary adjustments. Finalise co-ordination with the rest of the make-up team.

13 Be there early on performance nights. Allow plenty of time to make up the masses for any grand opening scenes and to be able to concentrate fully on any particularly complicated characters.

14 Be well organised for any quick changes.

15 After the final performance, tidy up and collect everything together, noting any items which need replacement and returning wigs to hire companies.

16 Update stocklist and faces file.

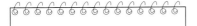

ALWAYS TAKE NOTES:

NEED MORE TRANSLUCENT POWDER & ROUGE

3 MENS WIGS TO RETURN.

JENNY HAS BORROWED THE CINDERELLA WIG

Analysis

Before beginning to organise the make-up, factors to consider are:

> **1**
> What is the style and period of the play?
>
> **2**
> How will make-up help to establish character?
>
> **3**
> Does any particular character need research or special attention?
>
> **4**
> Are there any fast scene changes that must be organised and practised in advance?
>
> **5**
> Who can help you to do the make-up?
>
> **6**
> Will any wigs have to be hired or bought?
>
> **7**
> What is the estimated cost of the make-up for this play?
>
> **8**
> What is the budget for make-up?

Type of play

Styles of make-up will vary according to the type of play and the approach to the production. Always begin by discussing the overall play with the director and others involved in its artistic interpretation so that everybody involved has a co-ordinated approach to the style of the play.

There are many types of play – for example:

musical

revue

fairy story or pantomime for children

thriller

melodrama

classical play

drawing-room drama

history drama

farce or comedy

plays in a specific setting, such as a hospital, school, monastery, court-room

Decide first if the type of play needs a special approach to the make-up. For instance, a fantasy for children or a melodrama will probably need 'over the top' make-up, while a British court-room drama will require most of the characters to have straight make-up – but will need a good number of wigs organising!

Characters and actors

Preparation for the make-up should begin well in advance of the performances, with the analysis of the characters and the kinds of make-up needed. This may involve some research, both into the attributes of the roles and the play's setting and into the specific make-up techniques that will be needed to achieve the right effects. The dedicated make-up artist will have books on the subject but may need to spend some time in the library checking up on other aspects – historic styles of make-up and hair, for example. Once the play

Analysis

has been cast then the make-up artist will be better able to judge how many make-ups are 'straight' and how many need special attention, such as:

1

Actors that need corrective make-up to alter their appearance appropriately

2

Actors that need to be made to look much older

3

Actors that need to be made to look much younger

4

Complicated make-ups that require time and practice, such as an animal or fantasy role – or a change of race and skin colour

5

Fast changes (these may be inherent in the plot – such as a dramatic moving forward or back in time – or they may occur if an actor has been cast in more than one role).

Points to check about characters

See also the section on Features on pages 13-15.

1

Race and skin type

2

Age – a vital factor

3

Temperament – for example a gloomy character will need more 'turned-down' lines; a happy one more 'laughter' lines!

4

Are there any special demands of the role: is the character described as being attractive and glamorous, or unattractive – ugly, even?

5

Are there any other special attributes: is the character described as good or bad, silly, humorous, or unwell?

6

Does the script indicate any special features – such as a large nose, long fingernails, tattoos, scars or a rosebud mouth?

7

Are any of the characters related to one another? Does this need to be shown through hereditary features?

8

Is any character famous – a familiar face already to the audience? For example, historic characters such as Napoleon, Royalty past and present, or a film star may need extra special study if any degree of authenticity is to be achieved

9

Occupation and lifestyle: certain occupations affect the skin – for example, a farmer or builder working outdoors will have a ruddier skin than someone who works, say, in an office; a coal miner may need to have his skin blackened; a wealthy aristocrat will look very different to a peasant in the French Revolution

---

Setting: time and place

Time

Historic details will require careful research. Even in recent times, there have been many changes in styles and the conception of what is considered beautiful alters too, from one generation to another.

Generally, the play's intent is to capture the 'feeling' of a particular period and the make-up artist will need to discuss the style of the production with the director before deciding on how to approach the make-up. For example, is the make-up and hairstyling to be a realistic duplication of the cosmetics and hairstyles used in the 1920s or should it emulate our impression of the Roaring 20s – which may be a different thing altogether!

As well as the century or decade, the time of the year may affect skin tones and the kind of make-up used from one season to another.

Even the time of day in certain scenes must be a consideration. Obviously, a character will need very different make-up if dressed up for a dinner party at 8pm than if tumbling out of bed the following morning! It is vital that the make-up artist reads the script thoroughly and is aware of these important factors.

Place

The setting needs to be taken into account, too. Each play script will include a description of the settings – for the play as a whole and for the individual scenes.

Check these carefully and note factors such as the following:

List out those settings or scenes that are significant. Often, the play may be set entirely in one place and all the characters can be treated as being in a single environment. If, however, the setting moves from, say, a palace to a dungeon or from city office to country cottage, these factors must be listed against the characters involved.

Planning for the performances

There are several factors dictated by the play and the order of appearances of characters. Work out beforehand some estimate of the time involved.

Take into account how much time is required prior to 'curtain-up'. How many people need to be made up for the opening or the earliest scenes? Who has fast changes and when? When do lots of people need help at the same time?

Then list the make-up needed in order of appearance. Decide which characters need expert attention and which can be managed by the actors themselves or by helpers. Define exactly where the pressure points will be.

Lists and plots

Overall production requirements

Play title

Play type

Date(s) of setting

Place(s) of setting/Time(s) of day

Time(s) of year

Play style

Who is in opening scene?

Special requirements

The forms on these pages 31-33 are free of copyright restrictions and are available to be photocopied.

Overall production requirements

Play title   *ABSOLUTELY KILLING!*

Play type   *THRILLER/COMEDY*

Date(s) of setting   *1920s*

Place(s) of setting/Time(s) of day   *SMALL 'ALMOST-STATELY' HOME*

EVENING DINNER (7PM); GARDEN PARTY (2PM); THE LIBRARY 11AM

Time(s) of year   *SUMMER*

Play style   *FUN/ESCAPIST; O.T.T.*

Who is in opening scene?   *MABEL, SHEILA, BARRY (AND ROSE APPEARS SCENE 2)*

Special requirements   *SCAR FOR RODNEY*

MABEL MUST LOOK ILL IN FRST TWO ACTS

BIT OF A RUSH FOR GARDEN PARTY CROWD SCENE – MAY NEED HELP

Make-up chart for women or girls

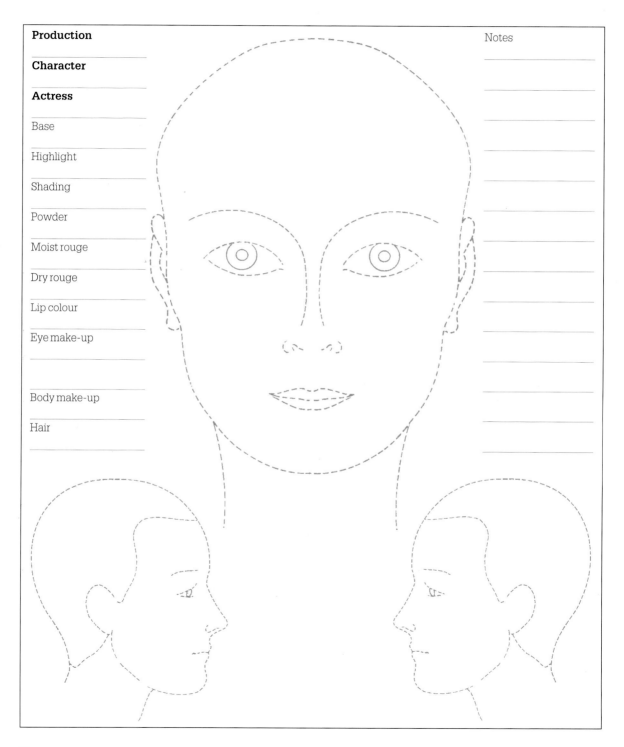

Production

Character

Actress

Base

Highlight

Shading

Powder

Moist rouge

Dry rouge

Lip colour

Eye make-up

Body make-up

Hair

Notes

Make-up chart for men or boys

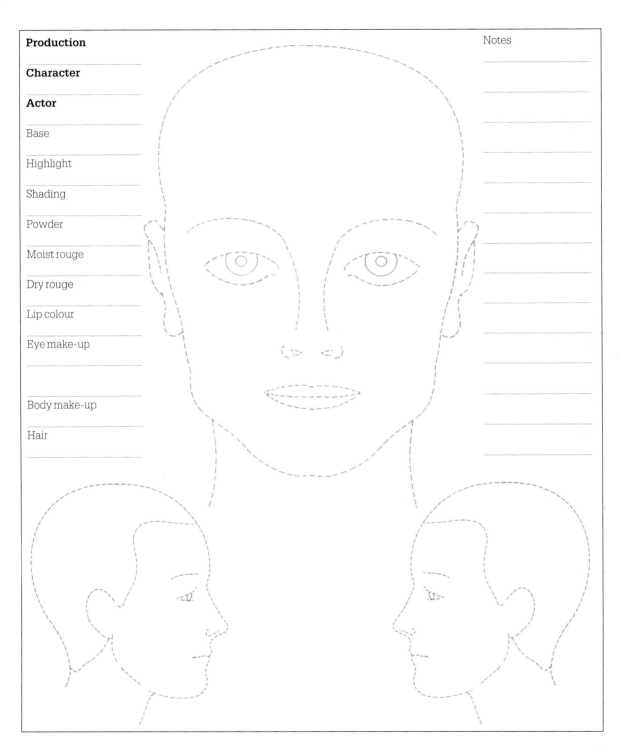

Production

Character

Actor

Base

Highlight

Shading

Powder

Moist rouge

Dry rouge

Lip colour

Eye make-up

Body make-up

Hair

Notes

Practice sessions

Individual character requirements

Name of Actor/Actress

Character

Basic appearance

Any changes needed

Fast change(s) on page(s)

Notes on eye make-up needed

Is wig required?

Special effect notes

First appearance on page

Individual character requirements

Name of Actor/Actress   *JULIA*

Character   *LORNA ASHCROFT*

Basic appearance   *CLASSIC 1920s; PRETTY, CUPID BOW LIPS*

Any changes needed   *WET AND DIRTY IN AFTER FALLING IN LAKE*

(ACT 3 SCENE 1 PAGE 73)

Fast change(s) on page(s)   *N/A*

Notes on eye make-up needed   *SUBTLE*

Is wig required?   *NO . . . BUT NEEDS TO STYLE HER OWN HAIR*

Special effect notes   *N/A*

First appearance on page   *43 (ACT 2 SCENE 1)*

The forms on these pages are free of copyright restrictions and are available to be photocopied.

Practice sessions

A complicated make-up or a fast change make-up needs practice. First talk to the directors and the actors concerned about what is needed. Then – once the research has been done, the make-up is planned and the necessary make-up items have been purchased or gathered together – find a suitable time to try out all the required effects.

This might be done during rehearsals when the actor is not needed on stage or, better still, find a separate time slot altogether so that there will be no pressure to rush the job. Trial and error can extend the process and as the minutes fly by, the actor will become restless if his or her cue is suddenly imminent. Make sure that you have sufficient colours to find out what suits the role and the actor's skin. Check the make-up onstage, under the lights, and see how the effects look from the audience viewpoint.

Sometimes, if wigs are being hired, for example, it will not be possible to check the full impact until the last moment but if the make-up has worked well in isolation, it can only be bettered once the final elements and costume are in place too.

Dressing room

The dressing room needs lots of mirrors – large (one full-length, if possible) and hand mirrors. Lots and lots of good light is absolutely essential and running water is great if you can get it!. Make sure there is sufficient seating and plenty of refuse sacks (trash bags) or waste baskets. A few lighting gels may be handy in order to check that the make-up looks good under the right coloured light.

Group make-up

Group make-up

Organising group make-ups

> **Key factors to success**
>
> Plan well ahead.
>
> Establish a hard core of experienced make-up artists.
>
> Organise lots of helpers.
>
> Find out which actors are able to do their own make-up.
>
> Make clear lists of who needs what and when.
>
> Keep the make-up room tidy and very well-organised.

Finding the team

Organising make-up for groups needs good planning, especially if a large number of actors are involved. Otherwise chaos will reign and many of those taking part go on stage wearing a make-up that they feel is dreadful and, in consequence, they may give an embarrassed and inhibited performance.

A good number of competent make-up artists will help speed the flow of the exercise and achieve the best results. However, willing untrained enthusiasts should still be encouraged to help as there is a good deal they can do with the more simple procedures to help ease the work-load.

Also, find out which of the actors can do their own make-up. Many will have belonged to groups where this was the norm and others, although inexperienced, may well understand the procedures after being made up countless times and will be able to

deal relatively comfortably with straight make-ups – even if only the first stages. Every little bit helps.

The exact procedure to be adopted will vary according to the size of the cast, the number of competent make-up artists and what facilities are available for doing the work.

Basically, there are two ways of tackling the problem:

1 Complete individual make-ups

The first, and without doubt the most artistically satisfying method, is for each make-up artist to completely make up a number of specific characters – which should then be checked and approved by the make-up artist in charge of the overall effect. However, if vast groups are involved, this method requires a large number of good make-up artists and more than the usual supply of make-up and

equipment – since each artist will need his or her own kit to hand.

2 'Conveyor belt' make-up

It is often far more practical to use the 'conveyor belt' system, where each make-up artist is allocated a specific step in the make-up sequence. The performers move down the line of artists, having one step at a time added, until they reach the chief make-up artist at the end of the line – who checks the make-up and makes any final adjustments or corrections. This method is excellent for straight make-ups but still needs to be carefully organised. Every performer should be given a chart, explaining exactly what make-up is required, which can

Group make-up

be shown to each make-up artist as the actor progresses down the line.

Ideally, there should be one or two helpers or assistant stage managers, who make sure that there is always someone ready and waiting to be made up and then also ensure that those not required are kept clear of the make-up area.

Complicated character make-ups

The more difficult character make-ups should still be done individually, since to create a convincing character, the make-up artists will need to see the work through from start to finish. These detailed make-ups should be allocated to the more experienced members of the make-up team, leaving the 'conveyor belt' to willing (but often untrained) helpers, who can easily apply a straightforward base or blusher.

The group make-up area

Having decided just how the make-ups are to be done, the next important thing to take into consideration is the make-up area. This should, ideally, be a large airy room with sufficient space to accommodate all the make-up team and a good number of the actors in comfort. Preferably this area should be situated fairly close to the stage itself, so that if any retouching or make-up changes are required during the performance, the actors do not have to rush around in a panic.

There should be sufficient well-lit mirrors, make-up tables and chairs for each of the make-up artists to have a separate working area and, if possible, a supply of running water. Finally, ensure that each make-up artist has a bag or waste basket ready for the disposal of used tissues and cotton balls.

Fast changes

Quick-change make-up

When a make-up has to be changed during the course of the performance, this often has to be done at speed.

Careful planning and, in some cases, a complete change from normal techniques may be required to deal with the situation. The kinds of make-up changes needed are so varied, there are no hard and fast rules to follow. However, here are a few points that should be remembered:

The forms on these pages are free of copyright restrictions and are available to be photocopied.

Quick change plan

Name of Actor/Actress

Character

Overall effect needed

When?

How long available?

Make-up changes:

Complexion

Eyes

Lips

Body

Hair/wig changes

Extras

Notes

Fast changes

1
The place where the make-up is done should be as close as possible to the stage.

2
Keep the make-up change as simple as possible, using the minimum of equipment.

3
Only those items required for the change should be on the make-up table.

4
Keep the various make-up items placed in the order in which they are to be used.

5
Rehearse the change to ensure that it is smooth-running, and feasible in the time allowed. If there are any doubts, then either the make-up change must be simplified or the flow of the script adjusted to permit more time.

Short cuts

There are also a number of short cuts that can be used with the equipment.

1
Try to choose those materials that can be applied directly to the skin – rather than those which are applied with brushes and sponges.

2
If brushes and sponges do have to be used, they should be already loaded with the required colours so that no time is wasted.

3
Brushes used for highlighting and shading should be colour coded on their handles for easy identification.

4
Keep all the brushes upright in containers, rather than left lying flat on the table, so that they are less likely to roll off.

5
If there are a number of changes during the play, someone specific should be put in charge of organising each change, laying out the equipment in the right sequence and loading the brushes and sponges so everything is ready and waiting for each make-up.

Quick-change methods

Depending on the type of change needed, there are a number of different techniques that can be used. Complete removal of the first make-

---

Quick change plan

Name of Actor/Actress *GILL PICKLES*

Character *SOPHIE LANCASTER*

Overall effect needed *LOSE 40 YEARS*

When? *PAGE 48 ACT 2 SCENE 2*

How long available? *6-7 MINUTES*

Make-up changes: *REMOVE WIG, SPECTACLES, AGEING LINES FAST!!*

Complexion *ADD CAKE FOUNDATION AND ROUGE*

Eyes *BLUE SHADOW; MASCARA; EYEBROW PENCIL*

Lips *CORAL PINK*

Body *NECK AND CHEST ALREADY DONE!*

Hair/wig changes *LONG BROWN WIG*

Extras *NECKLACE AND EARRINGS*

Notes *ABIGAIL WILL ASSIST US. CAN BE DONE AT SIDE OF STAGE IF WE KEEP ENTRANCE CLEAR FOR TERRY'S FAST EXIT.*

HIGH COLLAR OF 'AGED DRESS' HIDES NECK SO THIS CAN BE YOUNG ALREADY

IF ANY TIME LEFT FALSE EYELASHES, HIGHLIGHTS ON CHEEKS AND UNDER EYEBROWS

Fast changes

up is very time-consuming and should be avoided wherever possible. Cake make-up is invaluable for this because the colours can so easily be sponged one over another.

Changing complexion colour

Method one:
Using cake foundations
Simply sponge a new colour over the first make-up, using a slightly wetter sponge than usual. Remember, with cake make-up, that the foundation colour already on the skin is water-soluble so a certain amount of the colour will be picked up and mixed with the second application, affecting the final colour. If you need to lighten the skin tone, the second cake make-up should be lighter than the actual colour required – and vice versa if you need to darken the skin. Determine the colour to use by trial and error.

Method two:
Using grease and cake foundation together
For the first make-up, use grease or cream-stick make-up, which is thoroughly powdered. The skin tone can then be changed by sponging a film of cake make-up over the top.

Method three:
Using only grease foundation
When changing the skin tone, using only grease or cream-stick foundation, the first make-up should be left unpowdered to facilitate blending the second colour into the base.

Changing the details

When details such as eye make-up, lipstick or rouge need to be removed, do this before any other change is done. Make-up remover pads are ideal for this purpose, and a clean pad should be used for each detail so that none of the removed make-up is wiped back on to the face. Any excess removal oil should then be wiped off with a pad of cotton moistened with skin tonic.

If cake make-up is being used, the areas from which the original detail has been removed should be powdered first in order to ensure a really smooth new application.

Wigs, beards and moustaches

Wigs used for quick changes should be easy to put on and remove and need as little fixing as possible. They should be dressed in a style that cannot easily be messed up.

Prepared beards and moustaches should be used. Make sure they are on as strong a foundation as possible to prevent damage. For very quick application or removal, double-sided adhesive tape can be used but these hairpieces will stay in place only for a short time. Also, great care should be taken to place the hairpiece in exactly the right spot; if it has to be pulled off and readjusted, the adhesive quality of the tape is badly impaired.

Co-ordinate with the wardrobe department

When a make-up change is needed, there will, almost always, be a change of costume as well. So it is imperative, when planning the make-ups, to work in close conjunction with the wardrobe department to ensure that there is sufficient time for both types of change. Remember that the style of costume may help to give a strong indication of the age and temperament of the character. Often a very complicated make-up change can be avoided if the costume change conveys a strong enough message.

Plotting quick changes

To achieve a series of quick changes while remaining calm and efficient, you will need to plan ahead carefully, make clear notes and plot the make-up details logically.

1 List the changes needed in order, noting act, scene and page numbers in the script.

2 Detail under each change exactly what effect is required and which types and colours of make-up will be needed.

3 Estimate the available time and note this down.

4 Decide if the make-up needs to be done close to the stage because of tight timing.

5 Decide who is doing what.

To sum up . . .

Begin thinking about the production early, make sure all the make-up stock and equipment is organised in good time, do any necessary research and draw up sketches, lists, plots and charts as required. Talk to the directors, the cast and to lighting and wardrobe. Have practice run-throughs for complicated make-ups and for fast changes.

The key to successful stage make-up lies as much in good organisation as in artistic skills. It does not matter how brilliant the effects achieved if only half the required cast are ready to go on stage at curtain up. Careful planning will give both make-up team and actors time to enjoy the exciting visual changes that are possible and help them to make the most of this important element of character portrayal.

Make-up techniques

Applying the make-up: techniques

The stock is bought and the make-up kit is ready and waiting. The script has been studied and any specific research is underway. A plan of campaign for the performances has been devised and teams of enthusiastic would-be make-up artists have agreed to come along to help in whatever way they can.

So far, so good . . . but to make the most of all this organisation, the techniques for applying the make-up must be properly undertood and practised.

If the make-up artist is a total novice, it will be a good idea to buy at least one good book on the subject and to borrow more from the library. There is a lot to learn – and once the theory has been absorbed, it will help to practise the techniques on a willing victim before launching into the real thing for the peformances.

Most of the conventional techniques are not especially difficult but the more experience acquired, the better and faster the applications will become – and speed is often a fundamental factor.

Even the knowledgeable make-up artist will improve through reading up on the subject, refreshing his or her understanding of the techniques and learning about any new products.

Some professionals, theatre companies and organisations run classes and workshops on stage-make-up and these can be very stimulating to both expert and novice alike.

If new or more complicated techniques are to be applied, such as building a different shaped nose or creating a bleeding wound, some extra research and practical experimentation before the production run will certainly help achieve better results and will give both the make-up team and the actors a good deal more confidence about the procedures.

Preparation

In the whirl of pre-performance excitement and tension, it can be all too easy to rush the make-up. Calm careful preparation and application will help the actors to relax and get into character. Take each stage in logical order and do not panic!

Women should first thoroughly cleanse off all their day make-up. The skin should then be toned with a gentle skin tonic. If the skin is very dry, apply a small amount of an under-make-up moisturiser.

Men should ensure that they are clean shaven. At the dress rehearsals, remind the actors to try and shave at least an hour before the performance.

If the actor or actress has very oily skin, excess grease is best removed with skin tonic, or an after-shave lotion, on a moist cotton ball. Try to organise the actors and actresses to clean and prepare their faces before presenting them to you! This will save precious time.

Check the make-up charts and any notes or lists to make sure that you are absolutely clear what is expected and whether there are any special needs or complications (such as a strong lighting effect that might change the make-up colour). Some protection or cover-up of the clothes or costume will be needed. Then the hair should be drawn back and held back in place by a hair-band unless it is very short.

Help the actor to relax, make sure he or she is comfortable – and then, when you are both ready, the make-up application can begin.

Base

Once the skin is clean and prepared for action, the first requirement is to apply a base. This base color is the foundation upon which the rest of the make-up will be created so it is vital to use the right color and the right type of make-up for the particular role and skin type.

Hard greasepaint

1 First apply a thin film of cold cream to the skin to make blending easier.

2 Apply a few light strokes of the base colour on to the forehead, face and throat.

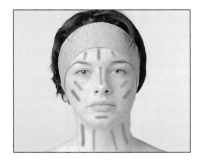

3 Using the tips of the fingers, gently blend the colour over the entire face and neck.

4 Fade the base colour away up into the hairline; try not to get any onto the hair itself.

5 When mixing two or more colours to make a new colour, apply alter-

Preparation and Base

nate dabs of colour to the face and blend them together with your fingertips. Do not blend one colour first and then try to apply the second colour over the top; this will give a heavy masklike finish.

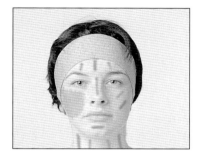

Soft greasepaint

1 Make sure the skin is completely dry and free from grease.

2 Squeeze the greasepaint onto the palm of the hand. Or, if the paint is packaged in a jar, transfer it with a spatula into your hand. Try to judge the amount so that you have just enough in your hand to complete the make-up.

3 Using a fingertip, put small dots of the greasepaint evenly all over the face and throat.

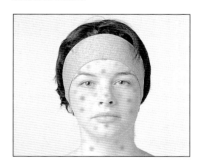

4 To mix a new colour, place the colours in the palm of your hand and stir them together with a fingertip before dotting on to the face.

5 Now blend the colour gently and evenly all over the face and neck – with your fingertips or a damp cosmetic sponge. Make sure that you cover all exposed areas of skin.

6 Gently fade the colour up into the hairline.

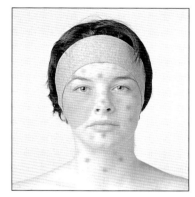

7 Rub a clean fingertip over the surface – if you leave a track or there is a lot of colour on your finger, you have used too much. Do not scrub the base directly off the face or the make-up will look patchy and uneven. Instead, blend once more, using all four fingers, until you have picked up a layer of the greasepaint; remove this from your fingers with a tissue. Continue until you are no longer picking up excess colour from the face.

Cream-stick foundation

This comes in a very wide range of skin tones so it is rarely necessary to mix them. Just choose the particular shade you need.

1 Apply the cream stick directly on to the face with broad stokes, using the cream base very sparingly.

2 Blend these strokes into a fine even film over the entire face and throat with a damp cosmetic sponge.

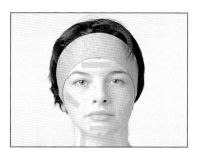

3 If you need to add more base to conceal shadows under the eyes or broken veins, pick up extra colour from the stick directly on to the sponge and then gently pat and stipple the cream over the blemish.

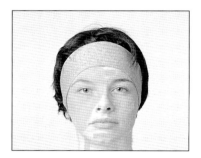

Liquid make-ups

These are generally water based and need to be applied with a dry cosmetic sponge. A damp sponge tends to dissolve the base and make the skin look patchy.

1 Decant a small amount of the liquid into the palm of your hand.

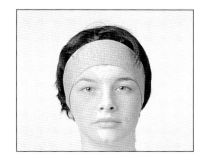

Rouge

2 Dip a corner of your sponge into the product and apply to the face.

3 Using a light stroking movement, blend it over the face and throat until a flawless finish is achieved.

4 Extra cover can be obtained by patting and stippling the liquid onto the areas concerned.

Rouge

After you have applied your foundation, the next step is to apply your moist or cream rouge. For a classic rouge application:

1 Pick up a small amount of the rouge on the tip of your forefinger and apply three dots of colour along each cheekbone. Start on the high point of the cheekbone and work backwards along the bone towards the top of the ear.

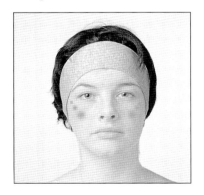

2 Now, with a clean finger, blend these three dots into a line of colour along the cheekbone; use small semicircular movements.

3 Wipe the finger clean and blend this line of colour away at the edges to produce a soft suffusion of colour over the cheekbone; do not take the colour too close to the nose.

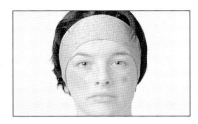

4 If you need to add more colour, repeat this process, starting once again on the highest point of the cheekbone.

Shadows and highlights

Once the rouge has been blended, it is time to remodel the face, as required, with highlights and shadows (see also pages 20-21).

The best brush for large areas, such as the temples or cheek hollows, is the 9mm (0.375 inch) square-ended sable. For lines and wrinkles use the 6mm (0.25 inch) square-ended type.

1 Apply colour with the brush and blend it away with this.

2 Carefully do the final blending with your fingertips, using light, stippling pats.

3 Highlight these shadows. As before, use first a brush and then your fingers.

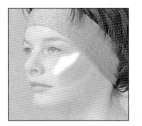

These highlights and shadows can be achieved in several ways. You can use lining colours. Alternatively, you can use colours chosen from the same range as your base. In this case, the highlights should be about four shades lighter and the shadows about four shades darker. It is impossible to do the shading this way with liquid make-up as the range of colours available is too limited.

Powder

Pick up a generous amount of powder on your powder puff (which should be of the flat velour type), fold the puff in half and rub the powder back into the fibres of the puff, leaving no excess on the surface. Now pat and press the powder into the make-up with a firm rolling movement of the puff.

Start on the throat at a point just below one ear and pat around the face in a decreasing circle, gradually working towards the nose which should be

Cake make-up

left until last. Never rub or smear the powder with your puff, as this will simply rub off the make-up.

1 Pick up powder on puff.

2 Fold powder puff sides together to enclose powder.

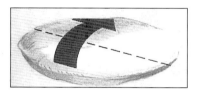

3 Rub powder well into the fibres of the powder puff.

Just before you powder the area around the eyes, make quite sure that the make-up is completely smooth and has not squeezed into any little lines and creases. If it has, then pat the make-up smooth with your fingertips and then powder this area immediately, to prevent this lined appearance reoccurring.

This creasing of the make-up around the eyes will occur on even the youngest face, but on an older face

there may also be lines on the forehead, in the fold between the nose and mouth and at the corners of the eyes, where the laugh lines are sometimes quite pronounced.

In these cases, gently stretch the lined area of skin between the first two fingers until the lines are flattened. Then pat the make-up smooth and thoroughly powder these areas while the skin is still taut. This will prevent the make-up 'cracking' into these lines after it has been on for a while. Otherwise the warmth of the skin could melt any unpowdered make-up.

When using hard or soft greasepaint, always remember to powder copiously, repeating this powdering process two or three times to ensure the make-up will remain set throughout the performance.

Cream-stick and liquid make-ups require less powdering, but this does not mean that the powder should be skimped. Any excess powder which is not absorbed by the make-up can always be whisked away with a face-powder brush.

Cake make-up

Cake make-up is applied with a moistened cosmetic sponge. The best type is about three inches (75mm) in diameter and should be made of fine-textured foam plastic.

1 Dip the sponge into a bowl of water, squeeze it gently until it is just short of dripping and then work it over the surface of the cake in a circular movement until you obtain a soft creamy texture. Take up enough of the colour from the cake to cover the entire face and throat. Then, working

quickly, stroke it lightly and thinly over the broad areas of the face, forehead, cheek, chin and neck.

2 Fold the sponge in half around your forefinger and, using the small area of sponge under the fingertip, fill in the areas around the eyes, the nostrils and the corners of the mouth. Squeeze out all the surplus water from the sponge, turn it over and use the clean side to carefully blend the make-up into a really smooth flawless finish.

3 Still using the clean side, blend the colour on the forehead up and into the hairline, taking care not to carry too much colour on to the hair itself. Fade the colour down the throat to avoid a masklike line where the make-up finishes.

4 Remember when choosing your colour of cake make-up to pick a shade that looks several tones darker on the surface than the colour you wish to achieve on the skin. If you do it this way you will find that the thinnest possible film of make-up will give you the correct colour and the most natural finish.

Powder

It is not normally necessary to use face powder over cake foundations since they dry with a matte finish anyway, but sometimes, when the skin tends to be over-greasy, a light powdering can be beneficial.

Retouching cake make-up

If necessary, cake make-up can be retouched using a small amount of the base colour on your sponge, but great care must be taken not to obliterate any detail of the make-up when doing so.

Cake make-up

Rouge with cake make-up

There are two methods of applying rouge with a cake make-up, using either moist rouge or dry cake rouge.

Moist rouge should be applied directly to the skin, using a stronger intensity of colour than usual and then applying cake make-up over it. This method is especially useful because it gives the very natural effect of the blush appearing to come from beneath the skin.

Dry rouge can be applied over the top of the cake make-up, using either a rouge mop or the small puff sometimes provided with the product. Using your sponge and what is left of the cake colour on it, blend the rouge softly into the foundation.

Most make-up artists prefer this second method as there is more control over the finished depth of colour. However, do experiment with both of these methods until you decide which suits you best.

Highlighting and shading with cake make-up

Method one

1 First apply chosen base and shadows.

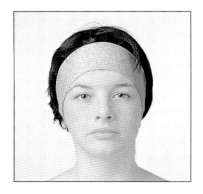

2 The highlights are then added, using a cake make-up that is several shades lighter.

3 These highlights and shadows area applied with either a 6mm (0.25 inch) or 9mm (0.375 inch), flat sable brush, depending on the size and type. Should any of these details dry before you have finished blending, just wet the brush or finger with a little water and then continue the blending.

Method two

1 First apply your shadows and highlights directly on to the skin, using grease lining colours. The shadows should be made with a very dark shading colour and the highlights a pure white.

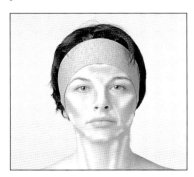

2 Powder these highlights and shadows with translucent face powder or white talcum.

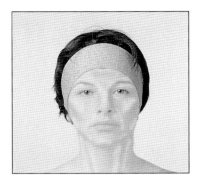

3 Then apply a thin film of your chosen colour of cake make-up over the top. You will not smudge the lining colours, providing that you remember to thoroughly powder them before applying the cake make-up.

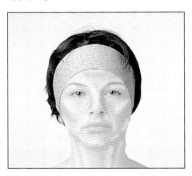

This method is particularly effective in small theatres or theatres in the round where a high degree of subtlety is needed, since the character work really seems to be 'under the skin'.

Eye make-up

Eyebrow pencil

A pencil sharpener will suffice if time is short but the best method of sharpening is to use a razor blade with only one cutting edge and a hard back. Press the blade into the wood of the pencil. At the same time, pull back the pencil with the fingers, so that the

43

Eye make-up

hand holding the blade only regulates its angle.

Slowly pare away the wood but do not allow the blade to cut into the wax. Gently scrape the wax down into the shape of a tiny, two-edged, flat-bladed sword. The point now has two sharp edges which can be used to sketch small hairline stokes into the brows and also to draw soft broad lines, using the flat sides.

If time is short, a pencil sharpener will suffice but it is harder to achieve a fine point without the lead breaking.

Use only tiny hairlike strokes, remembering to lift the pencil away from the skin at the end of each stroke to simulate the natural growth of the brow.

Eyeshadow

The number 6 filbert and the 6mm (0.25 inch) square-ended sable are the most useful brushes for eyeshadow. Use a separate brush for each colour. Otherwise the colours will mix together and turn grey.

If grease liners, cream-type shadows, or soft, cosmetic eye pencils are used, then they must be powdered to prevent creasing.

Powder shadows can be used on their own, but it is very difficult when using two or more colours together to prevent them smudging into each other and becoming grey.

Using a combination of cosmetic eye pencils and powder eyeshadows is the best technique.

The eye pencil is first applied to the eyelid in the pattern required and then set with powder eyeshadow, applied with a 6mm (0.25 inch) square-ended

brush. This type of application is very long lasting and, by using a mixture of different colours, very subtle colour combinations can be achieved.

1 Apply cosmetic pencil.

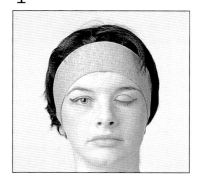

2 Blend out pencil with a blusher and soften edges.

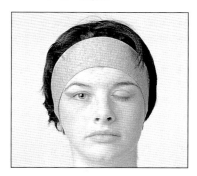

3 Apply powder eyeshadow to set.

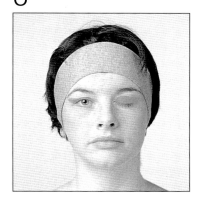

Eyelining

The eyes can be outlined using either a cosmetic pencil or a fine lining brush. The brush should be loaded with grease lining or water-soluble cake liner.

The finished eyeline must, however, be powdered and all too often the result can turn out looking smudged and dirty. Therefore cake or liquid liners are the best products to use.

fill the brush with colour and then draw the hairs to a fine point, thereby removing excess colour.

1 Starting at the inner corner of the eye, draw a line close to the roots of the lashes. Follow the curve of the lid to a point just past the outer corner of the eye. Extend the line at the end of the eye up and out, as illustrated.

2 Now line the lower lid.

In a large theatre, eyelines should be drawn clearly and sharply, but in more intimate settings they look more natural if they are slightly softened with the tip of your little finger or a clean sable brush.

Finishing touches

Mascara

1 Apply the mascara generously on to the lashes, ensuring that the colour goes right down to the roots of the lashes.

2 Allow the first coat to dry and apply a second coat in the same way, repeating this until you have sufficient colour on the lashes.

To make up the lower lashes, tuck your chin down as you did for the eyeliner and apply the mascara, using a sideways movement of the brush. Then brush downwards to separate the lashes. If your mascara is slow drying, it pays to make up the lower lashes before the top ones, so that when you look up into the mirror you don't smudge the colour on to the browbones in little dots of black.

Kohl

Kohl should not be applied until the mascara has completely dried. Look down into the mirror and gently pull the lower lid away from the eye with a fingertip. Apply the colour with a cosmetic eye pencil or grease lining on a 3mm (0.125 inch), square-ended brush. It is sometimes very effective to line the inside edge of the top lid, below the upper lashes.

> ### Finishing touches

Lip colour

1 Use a lip brush to achieve a clear clean out line. Brushes sold as lip brushes are square ended and very slightly larger than 3mm (0.125 inch), but these are generally too small. A number 6 filbert is better.

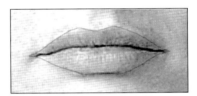

2 Always fully load the brush with colour. Work your brush over the lipstick or lining colour until the hairs are completely filled with the colour, then stroke the brush into an even shape to enable you to draw a clear outline.

Practise drawing lip shapes on the back of your hand to give you the feel of the brush. Use the side of the brush rather than the tip and always remember to keep the head of the brush inside the lip shape.

Keep your mouth in a relaxed shape (not fully open, however, as this distorts the shape) and draw on the outline, working from the corners of the mouth inward toward the centre. When your outline is complete, fill in the centre of the lips and gently blot the mouth with a tissue to remove any excess colour.

When overpainting the lips to enlarge the mouth, the outline can be drawn with a darker lip lining pencil than your chosen lip colour. If you need a very hard look to the mouth, leave this as a sharp line.

For a softer effect, carefully blend the line with a brush in toward the centre of the lips before filling in with the main lip colour.

When a very soft unpainted look is required, especially for some male make-ups, the colour should be applied very sparingly. Use the tip of your little finger.

Cake rouge

Once the make-up is completed and the lip colour added, the original application of rouge may seem a little weak. This can be heightened by the addition of a touch cake rouge at the last moment. This is applied with a rouge mop, using small semi-circular movements over the cheekbone, starting on the highest point and working back towards the top of the ear. Some corrective work can be done with cake rouge and this is described in fuller detail later.

Corrective make-up

Corrective make-up

This frequently means making the performers look more attractive – and younger! Before correcting a face, the make-up artist needs to discover its faults. To do this the artist needs to have a clear idea of just what is considered to be classically beautiful or good looking.

The classic face

There are two principal attributes to an ideal face – healthy-looking skin and harmonious proportions of the features (see also page 53).

Features of good health

Ideally, a normal oval face should be not too fat and not too thin; the skin should be smooth and elastic, without blemishes. A pink, even complexion indicates good health. The eyes should be open to normal degree and be clear and bright; the lips should be red and the cheeks rosy.

Harmonious proportions

Faces can be divided horizontally into three equal parts:

1
From the hairline down to the eyebrows

2
From the eyebrows to the tip of the nose

3
From the tip of the nose to the base of the chin

The face can also be divided vertically into five equal parts, with each part the width of an eye, and with the eyes the width of one eye apart.

The mouth should be just slightly wider than the width of an eye so that if imaginary lines were drawn vertically from the corners of the mouth they would just cross the inner edge of the pupils.

The nose should be straight, set in the exact centre of the face and neither too broad nor too narrow.

The eyebrows should be slightly arched and just a little less than one eye's width apart. The eye sockets should not be too deeply sunken.

Complexion

The state of the skin is the first thing to consider when applying a corrective make-up. If the complexion looks clean, healthy and perfectly unblemished, all that will be necessary is a light film of foundation, complimentary to the natural colouring of the performer and with sufficient strength of colour to compensate for the effects of the lighting.

If, however, the complexion is uneven, sallow, ruddy or spotty, it must be corrected with a suitable foundation.

Uneven skin tones
These can be corrected with a slightly heavier application of a clean foundation colour, carefully stippled over the skin with a moist sponge. Men should take care not to make the complexion look too smooth and clear as this tends to destroy the masculinity of the face and gives too 'pretty' an effect.

Sallow skins
Sallow skins need a fine film of founda-

tion, complimentary to the natural colouring and then warmed by the addition of moist rouge stippled over the entire face. Start with a small amount of colour, gradually adding more colour until the required degree of healthiness is achieved, heightening the colour on the cheeks, chin and forehead.

Ruddy complexions which have broken veins
The complexion can be improved by using an olive-based foundation, applied evenly all over the face. Stipple the colour on with a moistened sponge and gradually add more foundation to the ruddiest areas of the skin. Many people who have broken veins on their cheeks are nervous about using rouge but, without it, the face looks flat and uninteresting. It is best to use a tawny shade of dry cake rouge, gently dusted on with a rouge mop over well-powdered foundation (so as not to disturb the camouflage). Place the colour well back along the cheekbone toward the ear to draw attention away from the cheek pad.

Under-eye shadows
These can be hidden, by using either a light coloured cream-stick foundation or one of the specially designed cover creams available. Apply the colour with a small sable brush directly on to

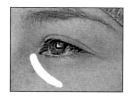

the shadow itself and then softly blend away the edges with the tip of the little finger until the highlight merges imperceptibly into the foundation. Take care not to get the highlight on to the puffy areas on either side of the shadow as this would make the shadow look deeper.

Spots and blemishes

These can be disguised by using the same products, but in this case the colour should not be lighter than your foundation as this would highlight the spot and make it look bigger.

Correcting facial proportions

If the horizontal and vertical divisions of the face are so unequal they upset the balance of the face, there are a number of ways these faults can be corrected.

Forehead

If the forehead is too high, it can be lowered by applying a fairly wide strip of shading colour along the top edge of the forehead, close to the hairline.

This band of shading can either be a foundation colour two or three shades deeper than the base or a dark-brown rouge colour. Blend the shading downwards on to the forehead until it merges into the foundation. The effect of this shadow can be heightened by dressing the front of the hair forward so that the lighting casts a shadow on to the top of the forehead.

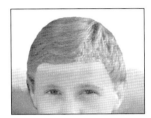

If the forehead is too low, it can be heightened by applying a highlight along the hairline. The hair should be dressed well back. This will allow the light to catch the highlight and make the forehead appear larger.

Too wide a forehead can be narrowed by simply shading the temple areas. Use a tawny shade of rouge, since brown shadows in the temples tend to add age to the face. Too narrow a forehead can be widened by highlighting the temple areas. This effect is also useful if you need to give a more youthful appearance to a face where the temples have become sunken with age.

If the forehead is too prominent, the whole area should be shaded with a darker base, fading the colour away as it reaches the temples.

Jawline

To strengthen a weak jawline, create a shadow immediately under the bone, fading it down on to the throat. Note the almost right-angled shape of the shadow applied just below the ear. A straight shadow here would be wrong as it gives a lantern-jawed effect.

Use shading to improve a weak jawline

A sagging jawline can be corrected by highlighting the depressions and shading the jowls. If the jawline and throat have dropped badly, very little can be done with highlight and shadow. In this case temporary facial lifts should be used. The construction and use of these types of facial lifts is explained on page 109 of *Create Your Own Stage Effects*.

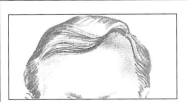

Shade hairline and dress hair forward to lower a high forehead

Highlight hairline and to dress hair well back to heighten a low forehead

Shade the temple to narrow a wide forehead

Corrective make-up

Neck

If the neck shows signs of age, you can shade the prominent muscles and highlight the depressions, but this must be done with great care. One simple trick is to use a foundation that is two shades deeper than the colour of the face. Apply this over the whole neck area.

Nose

Too long a nose can be shortened by applying a shadow under the tip and blending the edge up over the tip.

Too short a nose is lengthened by placing a highlight down the centre of the nose and carrying it down and under the tip, making the highlight strongest right on the point.

Too broad a nose is narrowed by shading down the sides of the nose and over the nostrils and then running a narrow highlight down the centre.

It is possible to make a bulbous tip to the nose appear much smaller by shading the tip on either side. Do take

care not to carry the shadow up the sides of the nose.

A sharp thin nose is the most difficult to correct. First run a broad highlight down the centre of the nose. Then very carefully pat a tiny amount of shadow just down the sharp bony ridge – to prevent the light catching it and so making it look sharper.

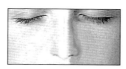

A broken or crooked nose can be corrected. Run a straight highlight down the nose, where it would be if the nose were straight and dead centre. Then shade it on either side.

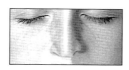

Chin

Too prominent a chin can be reduced by shading it with a dark foundation. A receding chin can be brought forward by lightening it with a highlight.

Eyes

The eyes are the most expressive and mobile features of the face and one of the most important assets that an actor possesses. It is vitally important to ensure that they look as good as possible and are able to be seen quite clearly from every seat in the house.

Since the male and the female orbital sockets are different and an actress can use make-up more obviously than an actor, we will deal with their problems separately. As a general rule, remember that dark colours are recessive so eye make-up for small eyes should be kept light in colour. Also, if the eyes are too prominent, avoid highly iridescent shadows.

Eyebrows

The eyebrow creates a frame for the eye, clearly defining the area within which eye makeup is applied. There are changing fashions in eyebrows for women; they can be thin and arched, heavy and straight, gently curving and so on. One thing is constant, however, and that is that the brow must always harmonise with the eye make-up and the rest of the face.

While men's brows usually need little corrective make-up, there are a few rules that govern the shape of the basic well-balanced natural-looking female eyebrow. Generally, the eyebrow should start just above the inner corner of the eye. Brows that are too close together give a stern frowning look; those that are plucked too far apart give a vacuous empty look to the face and make the nose look thicker than it really is.

A perfectly shaped brow points inward toward the other, never dipping downwards toward the nose. It then follows the natural arch of the

Corrective make-up

Improving the eyes with make-up

Male
Normal average
eyes

Before

After

Male
Small eyes

Before

After

Male
Close-set eyes

Before

After

Male
Drooping eyes

Before

After

Female
Classically
lovely eyes

Before

After

Female
Small deep-set
eyes

Before

After

Female
Close-set
drooping eyes

Before

After

Female
Round
prominent eyes

Before

After

Female
Wide-apart
eyes

Before

After

browbone to a point that is about 12mm (0.5 inch) beyond the outer end of the eye, winging slightly upwards at the outer end to prevent a downward droop – which would tend to age the face.

1 Hold the eyebrow pencil upright alongside the nose, with the point touching the browbone just above the inner corner of the eye. Ideally the eyebrow should start here, so mark this spot carefully.

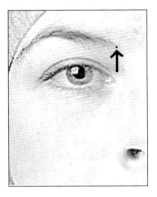

2 Hold the pencil diagonally, from the side of the nostril alongside the outer corner of the eye. This is where the brow should end. Mark this spot.

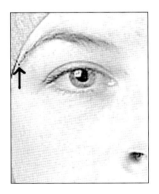

3 To determine the high peak of the eyebrow, hold the pencil upright over the outer corner of the eye and mark the spot.

Corrective make-up

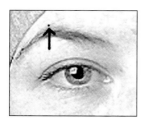

4 Using these three dots as a guide, lightly sketch in the shape of brow you require. Surplus hairs that detract from this shape can be plucked away from beneath the natural arch.

Blocking out the eyebrows
Simple but very effective changes can be made to eyebrow shapes with pencil, paints and brushes, especially if the natural brows are fair and not strongly marked. Sometimes, the natural browline must be blocked out before a new shape can be drawn – very useful for character make-ups.

There are several methods of doing this. The first is to rub a moistened bar of soap over the brows until they are flattened to the skin. Allow soap to dry and then cover brows with a thick coat of greasepaint and powder. This method is unsatisfactory for several reasons: first, the hairs can very quickly loosen and begin to show through during the performance; second, if the actor has very dark strongly-defined brows, these are almost impossible to hide; and lastly, if the stage is hot, perspiration can melt the soap, which may run into the actor's eyes and be extremely painful.

A safer method is to use a stick of Kryolan eyebrow plastic instead of soap, covering with greasepaint as before. However, this too can easily loosen and allow the hair to show.

The best method is to use a combination of spirit gum and Derma Wax. If this method is used, the Derma Wax will require careful removal afterwards. first peel off the film of sealer and then gently work make-up remover into wax. Remove it with a cleansing tissue. finally, dissolve the gum with spirit-gum remover, taking great care not to let it run down into the eyes.

1 Brush spirit gum into brows and comb hairs upward.

2 Once gum is tacky, press hairs down with a lintless towel. Apply Derma Wax and then sealer.

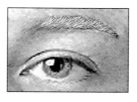

3 Cover with grease make-up and then translucent powder.

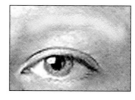

4 Now paint on new eyebrows using tiny hair line strokes to build up the new shape.

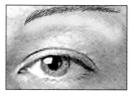

Once the natural brow has been blocked out, a new browline can be drawn on, but whichever method of blocking out is used, great care must be taken not to disturb any of the camouflaged hairs. Eyebrow pencils are generally too hard for this purpose and will tend to cut into the wax and make-up. So the safest method is to paint on the brows with a number 2 sable brush, using grease or cake lining colour. Build up the shape you require with tiny hairlike strokes of colour to simulate natural growth.

Cheeks and face shapes

If the face is a normal oval, neither too fat nor too thin, and you wish to make the face look as young as possible, then a classic rouge application is all that is necessary. However, if the face is either too fat or too thin, some corrective shading and highlighting must be used.

Slimming too full a face

1 Using your fingertips, trace the position of the cheekbone.

2 With either your finger or a brush, lay a line of colour along the underside of the bone from the ear to just under the high point of the cheekbone, slightly curving the line upward as you reach this point.

3 Soften the top edge of this shadow with a clean finger, brush or sponge, taking care not to carry the colour up over the top of the bone. Then blend the bottom of the shadow downward into the cheek hollow until it merges into the foundation.

4 Using a clean finger or brush, highlight the cheekbone, blending the upper edge so that it merges with the foundation and softening the

Corrective make-up

Optical illusions

Use shadows and highlights

Make-up depends on light and shade, on its sculpturing qualities, rather than just colour. For example, lines alone will not age a face convincingly. Instead use shadows and highlights to create the effect of sagging jaws, eyebags, or wrinkles. Light and shade will emphasize the contours of any three-dimensional shape, including the face.

Use optical illusions

1 Horizontal shadows and lines will widen and flatten a face.

2 Vertical shadows and lines will narrow and lengthen the face.

3 Lots of little divisions make a line look longer. So, in the same way, accentuating eyelashes with mascara makes eyes look wider.

4 Light areas always look bigger.

5 Dark areas always look smaller.

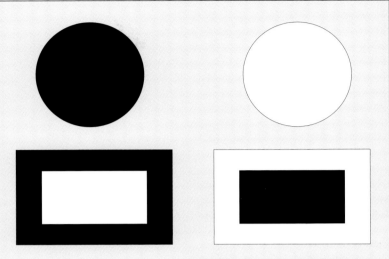

Black absorbs light so dark shapes seem smaller than light ones. This effect is exaggerated if a black shape is surrounded by white, and vice versa

Identical line lengths can appear shortened by enclosing them in angled lines and longer by using opening-out angles. Eye make-up reflects this

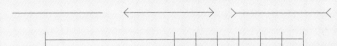

Little transversal dividing lines make the right half of this line seem longer

A face can be broadened by horizontal lines, whether in make-up or costume, and narrowed by vertical ones, as shown in these two characters

51

Corrective make-up

lower edge into the upper edge of the shadow. There should be no hard line between the two.

5 To give a softer and more glamorous effect on a female make-up, apply cake rouge after the highlights and shadows have been powdered. Keep the colour light over the highlighted area; intensify the colour in the shadow area. For a stronger effect, a dark shading rouge can be applied in the shadow.

Filling out too thin a face
If the cheek hollows are too sunken, a highlight two or three shades lighter than the base colour should be applied to the shadowed area below the cheekbone. Women should then apply a light dusting of rouge over the cheekbone.

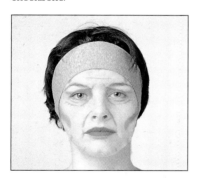

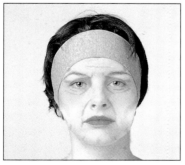

Teeth

Unattractive dark or discoloured teeth

or gold caps can be disguised with a light tooth enamel. However, great care should be taken to use a creamy shade that closely matches the good teeth – pure white tooth enamel will look grotesque.

If the teeth are uneven in length, the line can be straightened by using black tooth enamel on the tips of the long teeth. However, an effect like this can be used only in very large theatres. Since good teeth are essential to an artist playing anything but character roles, a visit to the dentist might be in order!

Mouths

Female mouths
Correcting the shape of the mouth is obviously much easier for women than for men since the lips can be boldly over-painted, or under-painted, with a strong lipstick colour to achieve the desired shape.

Male mouths
As a general rule the male mouth should be underplayed so correction may not be necessary. If it is needed, then care should be taken to make the lip make-up as natural as possible, using a brownish-red tone of lip colour or even a brown eye pencil.. Any corrections should be done as subtly as possible.

Thin lips
If the lips are too thin, draw outside the natural line of the lips but don't change the shape. This overpaint should be drawn on with a darker shade of lipstick or lip liner and the centre filled in with a lighter shade to give fullness.

Thick lips
If the mouth needs to be slimmed, apply your base cover over the outside edge of the lips and draw on a new outline just inside the natural rim, using a muted tone of lipstick.

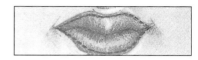

Small mouth
If the mouth is too small and narrow, then carry the colour right to the extreme corners, and just beyond on the top lip. Very slightly overpaint the whole bottom lip, following its natural shape.

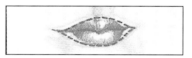

Droopy mouth
If the mouth has a heavy upper lip, a thin lower lip, and the corners turn down, overpaint the lower lip to meet the upper one and turn up the corners of the top lip with your colour.

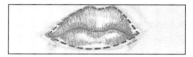

Too wide a mouth
If lips are too wide, cover outer corners with foundation: do not carry lip colour into corners.

Thin top lip
If upper lip is too thin or straight, add fullness until it balances lower lip.

Corrective make-up

Thin lower lip

If the lower lip is too thin, draw outside the lower lip to balance the top and highlight the centre of the lower lip with a pale iridescent lipstick.

Crooked lips

If the mouth is crooked, slightly underpaint the high side and slightly overpaint the low side – never do the correction on just one side.

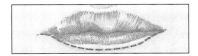

The classic face should have harmonious proportions. As described on page 46, faces can be divided vertically into five equal parts (each part the width of an eye) and horizontally into three equal parts:

1
From hairline to eyebrows

2
From eyebrows to tip of nose.

3
From tip of nose to base of chin.

If the shape of the face is not perfect, changing hairstyles can help to create the right balance.

Hair

Many facial faults can be disguised with cosmetics but hairstyles can help to alter the balance too. This is particularly true for women, but men can also benefit from rethinking their hairstyles. Some hints on corrective hairstyles are included here.

Square face before   *after*

Round-shaped face before   *after*

Pointed nose before   *after*

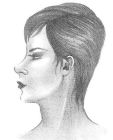

Heart-shaped face before   *after*

Short neck before   *after*

Prominent chin before   *after*

Who and how

Analysing the specifics

While the basics of make-up theory and technique remain the same, whatever the play or the actors involved, the approach and application are subject to a variety of considerations. For example, while light and shade will always be a major factor in the creation of an effective make-up, the heaviness of the application will need to be greater if the performance takes place on a large stage than when it is happening in a small intimate theatre.

In the same way, the type of person being made up will vary from the small child to the eighty-year old – with each age group needing its own level of make-up, while the make-up for men requires a quite different approach to the make-up for women; and people with darker skins require different treatment from those with pale skins.

This section aims to analyse the face, the 'canvas' on which the make-up will be applied – and the specific effect required for, more or less, conventional make-up. Exotic, ethnic and character make-up will be discussed in later sections.

Straight make-up for women

Really, there is no such thing as a straight make-up in the theatre – or for that matter, in any of the acting media – since every make-up should be designed to portray a character of one kind or another, however 'normal'.

Of course if an actress been cast 'to type', for both her acting ability and also for her physical appearance, then it will not be necessary to apply a

character make-up. But you will still have to use a make-up that is strong enough to offset the draining effect of the stage lighting and to define the features sufficiently well for them to be seen quite clearly from every seat in the theatre.

In addition to these practicalities, generally the actress will wish to look as attractive as possible to the audience. As none of us can claim to have physical perfection, every so-called straight make-up becomes, in effect, a corrective make-up.

Straight roles for women can vary from the woman who wears no make-up at all, or those who use just a dab of lipstick and a touch of eyeshadow, on to those who don a complete maquillage but still look natural by today's standards. Hopefully, earlier character analysis will have defined which make-up type the part demands.

The following step-by-step routine is planned so as to be adaptable to whichever degree of artifice is required to put the most appropriate face forward.

Colour guide

Foundation
Peach, creamy or light-tan groups

Rouge and lip colour
Light or medium-red groups

Highlights
Pale groups

Shading
Warm, brown shading colour

Eyeshadow
Neutral grey or brown for natural look, or a colour to harmonise with the costume

1 Prepare the skin and apply a smooth, light film of foundation.

2 Add moist rouge to cheeks and a touch of colour to browbone, forehead and chin.

3 Highlight and shade, then powder face well.

4 Reshape the brows with eyebrow pencil, using tiny hairlike strokes. Follow natural growth of brow.

5 Apply eyeshadow to the top lid, using a number 6 filbert brush. You should use a separate brush for each individual colour.

6 Draw in contour line with pencil or lining colour and blend away on to browbone with a 6mm (0.25 inch) flat-ended brush.

7 Outline the eye with eyeliner, being careful to keep the outer ends open as shown on page 48.

8 Mascara top and bottom lashes.

9 Apply lip colour with a number 6 filbert brush, doing any corrective work that is needed.

10 Strengthen cheek colour with dry cake rouge if needed.

11 Don't forget to make up the hands, too.

Straight make-up for a sophisticated city woman

1 Begin with a straight female foundation colour, or, if appropriate, make the character appear tanned.

2 Shade and highlight to improve the facial structure. Ensure that any tiredness shadows are disguised.

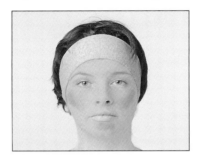

3 Powder with translucent powder.

4 Apply a powder shimmer that complements the eye colour, Apply this from the eyelashes to the eyebrows.

5 Line the eyes with a black liquid eyeliner. Keep the line narrow and extend the outer corners as in a straight make up, but drawing right round the inner corners.

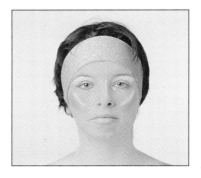

6 Feather a little more powder colour over the lids, leaving the centres white. Alternatively you can use pink or peach eye shadow.

7 Define the eye socket with a dark brown powder shadow, fading it onto the outer edge of the eyelid. Add iridescent powder shimmer to the centre eyelid and under the brow.

8 Apply at least two layers of black mascara and brush this through the lashes.

9 Use a brownish rouge in the hollows under the cheekbones and up over the temples.

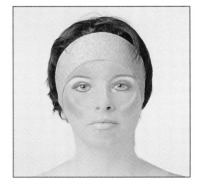

10 Outline the lips with dark red. fill them in with a medium-toned colour. Take a line of highlight under the outer corners of the lower lip. Then powder.

Analysing the specifics

11 Finish the effect with a sophisticated hairstyle or a wig with tints and volume.

Straight make-up for a country woman

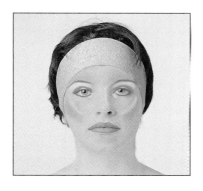

1 To suggest healthy-looking skin, choose a straight, not too pale, foundation.

2 Shade and highlight the eye area only (unless you are reshaping a naturally broad face or trying to reduce a large nose). Use the highlight as eye shadow

3 Ask the actress to smile. Paint highlight onto the contours created by the smile, blending these into a soft round shape.

4 Add top and bottom eye lines and socket shadows. Apply mascara to the eyelashes.

5 Brush through and colour the eyebrows; add a little Vaseline to unplucked brows and hair-like stokes to thin brows with a pencil or cake liner, following the natural hairs.

6 Draw some freckles on with a sharp brown pencil. Place the freckles across the nose, on the cheeks close to the nose and on the forehead; pat these carefully.

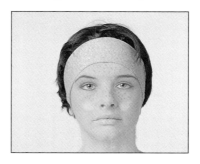

7 The lips need to look natural. Ideally, choose a peachy tone. On a small stage you may need no lipstick, or a very soft unobtrusive one so the lips look fairy natural.

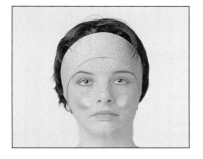

8 Finally, add rouge, using a warm rosy shade with no blue in it. Leave an area of pale highlight around the rouge application.

Straight make-up for men

Any ordinary male role will require a degree of make-up if the face is not to flatten under stage lighting. Everything that has been said about straight make-up for women applies equally to men, but a man's make-up must look completely natural and in no way over-made-up. So it is important to use as little make-up as possible but to gain the maximum effect from it.

Choose a foundation colour that looks much darker in the stick or cake than you think you need, and then apply the thinnest possible film of colour so that it gives a very natural and un-made-up look to the skin. At the same time, ensure that the colour flatters the natural skin tone.

Keep eye make-up to an absolute minimum. Only neutral browns and greys should be used for shadow, and eyelining should give the appearance of shadows rather than a hard line, except when the make-up is for a very large theatre.

Lips should be treated with great care since even the tiniest amount of lip colour can give a lipsticked appearance to the mouth. When lips are naturally well formed and strongly coloured, they are best left without any make-up at all, but if they do need colour, just the smallest amount of a dark brown-red, applied with the finger rather than a brush, will give a good natural result.

Rouge should be used to give the face shape rather than colour, placing it

Straight make-up for men

under the cheekbones, in the temple hollows and along the browbone.

If the face has a good bone structure, modelling is usually unnecessary since modern stage lighting is very flattering, so use modelling only when there is a need for correction.

In this step-by-step routine a certain amount of corrective modelling has been added – just how much of this is needed for the actor must be left to your discretion.

Colour guide

Foundation
Choose from light, deep and warm-tan groups or olive groups for Latin characters

Modelling colour
Use lake groups or choose from warm-tan or deep-brown groups.

Highlights
Use pale or ivory groups

Eyeshadow
Dark brown or greys

Lip colour
Dark-red or lake groups

1 Apply your chosen foundation to a clean-shaven and grease-free face. Remember to keep the foundation as light and natural-looking as possible.

2 Add modelling colour, using either a moist rouge or a warmer, deeper tone of your foundation.

3 Add corrective highlighting and shading where considered necessary. If grease or cream-stick foundation is being used, then the make-up must be thoroughly powdered at this stage. Cake make-up applications do not need powdering.

4 Where eyebrows need to be strengthened, sketch in with short hairlike strokes to simulate natural growth. Take care not to make the brows too dark or heavy.

5 Apply neutral eyeshadow to the eyelid, intensifying the colour in the contour crease.

6 Draw in eyelines, blending away the edges with a sable brush or fingertip. The larger the theatre, the stronger the lines. For small intimate stages they should be kept to the barest minimum. If the lashes are fair or poorly defined, a light coating of mascara can be applied, but take care not to make the lashes look over-made-up.

7 Apply lip colour, using a fingertip or brush. Make the top lip slightly darker than the lower lip. If the lips are naturally well formed, remove excess foundation from the lips.

8 Add cake rouge if the cheek colouring needs to be intensified.

9 Make up hands and all exposed skin, including the back of the neck which is so often neglected in a man's make-up.

Straight make-up for men

Straight make-up for a town or city man

1 Apply a straight foundation colour and shade under the cheekbones and down the sides of the nose.

2 Add the highlights onto the cheek bones and down the centre of the nose. Then shade the brow bones, unless the eyebrows are very heavy, and take a little around the inner corners of the eyes.

3 Highlight the eyelids.

4 Powder the whole face.

5 Using a pencil or a cake liner and brush, bring the eyebrows a little nearer to the nose, working upwards with small strokes. If you are using cake liner, check the colour on the back of your hand before you start. If you use a pencil, keep wiping the point on a tissue as you go, to remove any powder.

6 Line under the eye as usual and only mascara the top lashes.

7 Using a basic male colour, apply the rouge, slightly higher than usual and along the cheekbones, but not as far as the hairline. This adds to the lean look. Darken the lips slightly with a little brownish-red lip liner on a finger or brush. Don't use too much colour and don't go over the edge of the lips. (If the mouth is large and well coloured, leave out this step.)

Straight 'country' make-up for a man

1 Start with a tanned foundation, applied thinly.

2 Shade and highlight the eyes.

3 Trace shader into the tiredness lines under the eyes, into the smile lines and into the lines at the corners of the mouth.

4 Add highlights between the shadows and the eyes and on the cheek sides of the smile lines. Blend, and then powder carefully.

5 Unless the theatre is small and intimate, underline the eyes as for a straight make up and apply a little mascara.

6 Brush powder blusher across the forehead close to the hairline, down the centre of the nose and near the natural position for men, but a little closer to the middle of the cheeks.

7 Stipple a little brownish-red cream liner over the rouge and on the neck and chin with a finger or stipple sponge. Do not use too much or it can look like bruising.

8 Build the eyebrow shape with a pencil or cake liner, working among the natural hairs to make the brows look heavier.

9 Leave the lips natural.

Glamour on stage

The make-up techniques shown here are unashamedly artificial. The aim is to make the actress look as glamorous and beautiful as possible. These techniques are basically intended for use on very large stages for musicals and opera so they must be bold in design and strongly coloured to be in keeping with the costumes and scenery.

Do remember that the lighting for this type of production is usually very bright and colourful, so make sure that the foundation colour is very clear and strong too – and considerably warmer than the type you would use on a smaller stage.

Eye make-up should be strong and bright and very clearly defined.

False lashes give a glamorous look to the eyes but be careful with your choice of style. Very heavy dense lashes tend to cast dark shadows over the eyes and can make them all but disappear. Pointed lashes with well-spaced clumps are best.

Corrective highlighting and shading plays an important part in this type of make-up and should be used boldly and strongly.

Lip colour should compliment both costume and complexion but at the same time it must be strong, clear and bright. Soft subtle colours may look attractive at close quarters but will inevitably disappear under strong lights on a large stage. Lip gloss is also very useful for this type of make-up.

The general rule throughout is to use strong clear colours and warm tones. Be bold in design.

Colour guide

Foundation
Choose from the peach, creamy and light-tan groups

Rouge
Light and medium-red groups

Lip colour
Light or medium-red groups, or lipstick to harmonise with costume

Eyeshadow
To harmonise with natural eye colouring or costume. Iridescent colours are particularly good.

Black performers

Black performers

Apart from the actual skin colouring and in consequence, the selection of appropriate make-up colours to suit the black skin, all the basic principles already discussed apply to the black performer as well as to the white-skinned actor.

Black actors have one big advantage over their white counterparts in that very often the natural skin colour looks fine under stage lighting, without the use of foundation. All that is needed is a small amount of highlighting and shading to accentuate the features.

However, there are many more variations in the colouring of black skins than in white skins. These range from the pale coffee-coloured complexion, through yellowy and reddish browns, to the very dark black skin. It is when these colours need adjusting that certain difficulties may arise.

Since dark colours are recessive, very dark skins tend to make the features disappear on stage. It is necessary to lighten the skin tone so that the artist can be seen at his or her best – but often, when a dark skin is lightened, it looks dull and chalky and assumes a very dead appearance. This is because light-brown make-up has a great deal of white pigment added to make it light and this white pigment can give the black skin a chalky appearance.

So, when choosing a make-up for this purpose, make sure it contains strong yellows or reds, according to the natural colouring of the skin. These colours (which in the stick tend to look overbright and unnatural) are the most effective in lightening a black

skin, but the exact shade and colour required can be determined only by trial and error.

Conversely, a black actor with a light-brown complexion may sometimes need to darken the skin tone to suit the role. The resulting make-up sometimes makes the skin look dull and muddy. Avoid this by using a colour which, although darker, is also brighter, with more depth of colour than the natural skin.

When the skin tone is the right colour but the complexion is a little uneven, a normal make-up base may make the face look masklike. Use instead a 'face glosser' or 'gleamer'. These products contain a low level of dark pigment mixed with iridescent material which imparts an attractive gleam to the skin and, at the same time, evens out any patchiness in the complexion.

The general rule for black performers is to add brightness to the skin and this also applies when using cheek colour, eyeshadow and lipstick. Muted subtle colours tend to become muddy and disappear. Keep the choice of colours clear, clean and bright.

Straight make-up for the black actress

1 Study the skin colouring closely to determine whether it contains yellow or red undertones.

2 Then apply a foundation that is complimentary. On a yellow-toned complexion, use a bright golden-yellow tan. On a red-brown complexion, use a bright orange-red tan.

3 Keep the application as fine as possible to prevent a masklike appearance or use one of the face-glosser products.

4 Powder the make-up with a translucent face powder containing a small amount of iridescent material, which will help to retain the attractive gleam of a black skin.

5 If the brows are poorly defined, try sketching them in with black eyebrow pencil. Always use short hairlike strokes, as this will best simulate the natural growth.

6 Apply a clear, bright eyeshadow colour to the upper lid. All iridescent colours, including metallic golds and silver, are especially attractive on black skin.

Middle-aged women

7 Using very dark lining colours or eye pencils, draw in the contour crease, blending the shadow up and over the browbone at the outer end of the eye. (If the skin colour is particularly dark, black kohl pencil can be used for this contour shadow).

8 Clearly outline the eyes, using black lining colour. Paint the top and bottom lashes with black mascara. If the eyelashes are very short and sparse, false lashes can be used to good advantage, particularly when a very glamorous make-up is required.

9 Apply a strong shade of lip colour with a number 6 sable brush. If, however, the lips are overlarge, keep the outline just inside the natural shape and avoid using overbright or very pale colours, as these tend to enlarge the mouth.

10 Brush a bright, strong powder rouge over the cheekbone, adding a touch to the forehead and chin. Where corrective contouring is needed, a dark-brown shading rouge should be strongly applied under the cheekbone (before applying the normal cheek colour over the cheek area) and over the top of the shading rouge already applied.

11 Generally, there is no need for hand and body make-up, although occasionally the pigmentation on the hands can be broken and uneven, in which case body make-up should be used to correct this.

Straight make-up for the black actor

Corrective make-up for the black actor should be kept to the absolute minimum. Bear in mind that the foundation should be as fine as possible to avoid any suggestion of an over-made-up appearance.

1 Apply a fine film of foundation when needed, using light liquid foundations or face glosser. If the skin tones are uneven, a very thin film of a strong, bright cake foundation can be used but choose colours carefully and experiment first.

2 Eyebrows on the black male may be rather undefined and, although this looks natural at close quarters, it can look a little strange on stage. A slightly stronger amount of definition may be applied with a black eyebrow pencil, taking care not to overdraw the brows as this can give a comical look to the eyes.

3 Apply a highlight to the actual lid area and the browbone. This highlight should be some four shades lighter than the skin colour and contain golden-yellow tones. Metallic gold eyeshadow, used discreetly, can often work very well.

4 Darken the contour crease if needed, using very dark-brown or black pencil or lining colour. Fade the edges away, using a 6mm (0.25 inch) sable brush. Then outline the eyes with black pencil and soften away the edges, again using a 6mm (0.25 inch) sable brush.

5 If the lips lack definition and colour, a small amount of very dark brown-red rouge can be added with the fingertips. Be careful not to over-redden the mouth. If the mouth does look too red, add a touch of black pencil to tone it down.

Middle-aged women

Middle age is an undefined period of time between youth and say, about sixty-five years. How a woman ages depends on her lifestyle, health and how much or little she cares for her appearance. So before planning this

Middle-aged women

type of make-up, character analysis is vital. A mature actress playing a middle-aged character needs only to put on a make-up suitable to the character's way of life.

The following routine however, is designed to show a younger actress how to age her face when called upon to play a more mature character.

The first consideration should be what to do with the hair. A good wig, of grey or greying hair in a mature style, is usually the best solution but you may prefer to restyle and grey the actress's own hair. Or it could be decided that this character would colour her hair to look younger!

Once you have decided on the most apt approach, then try on a suitable wig or hairstyle – but with no make-up yet applied.

Colour guide

Foundation:
For warm, healthy middle age use peach or pink groups muted with a small amount of sallow or ivory groups
For pale sallow tones use sallow or ivory groups mixed with a small amount of peach or pink groups

Shading:
Use olive and lake groups

Highlights:
Use ivory or pale groups

Rouge and lips:
Dark or medium-red groups

Eyeshadow:
Dark-mauves, blue-greys, browns, dark-green or blue

If the skin is naturally pale and colourless, you may not need to use a foundation. The addition of shadows and highlights will suffice to give the right effect.

If, however, the skin still looks very youthful, you will need to apply a suitable foundation to drain away the bloom of youth.

1 Remove wig and apply foundation.

2 With the skin colour suitably adjusted, return the wig to its block and start to shade the face. Apply shadows where needed with a sable brush.

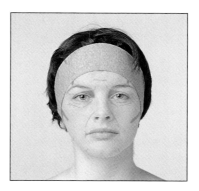

3 Blend out the shadows and apply highlights to give them depth and roundness. Now thoroughly powder the make-up.

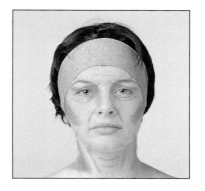

4 Use powder eye-shadows in ageing colours such as mauve or grey-blues. Keep eyelining and mascara to a minimum.

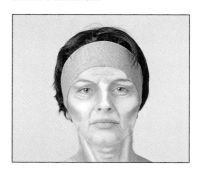

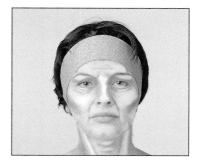

5 Apply a small amount of a dark, ageing lip colour, using a number 6 sable brush.

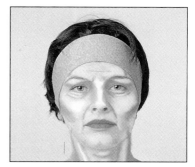

6 Restyle hair or replace wig, fastening in place with pins and clips. Secure wig lace with spirit gum.

7 Make up hands and all exposed skin areas to tone in with the face.

Middle-aged men

A man's appearance in middle age will vary according to his lifestyle, health, and his pride in his appearance. Study the character and analyse just how he is meant to look.

1 Then take a careful look at the hair and see what can be achieved with just a small amount of restyling. Dressing the hair back from the forehead will often reveal the early signs of receding hair. Add a touch of grey at the temples and maybe a moustache,

and you will often give sufficient maturity without resorting to a full character make-up. If the hair looks too youthful to be successfully restyled, however, then a good wig will be needed.

2 Shadows and highlights will need to be added to the face, together with a rather fuller moustache. Shadows and highlights around the eyes need particular attention, as well as the jawline and neck.

3 Middle-aged make-up for the fuller face does not rely so heavily on shadows and lines. More use is

made of broad planes of ruddy colour. The eye make-up can help to create a puffy look to the eyes.

A full beard round the sides of the face may help to create a suitable widening effect.

Colour guide

Foundation:
For sallow skin tones use creamy or sallow groups
For healthy skin tones use light-tan groups mixed with florid groups

Shading:
For sallow skins use olive-brown groups
For healthy skins use lake groups

Highlights:
Use ivory or pale groups

Eyeshadow:
Brown plus lake groups

Lip colour:
Use lake or florid groups

Thin old age

Thin old age

Advanced old age is usually characterised in the theatre by extreme thinness, since a very thin, bony appearance gives a greater illusion of age than one of fatness and obesity.

To achieve this effect, the skin must be made pale and parchment-like and appear to be draped over the bone structure. This will give the face a skull-like appearance. Men and women age in a similar manner so we can look at a step-by-step routine for a woman and then examine finished thin old-age make-up for both sexes.

1 Try on the wig and study the general effect on the actor's face. Then remove the wig and keep it on its block until all the make-up has been completed.

2 Apply a pale sallow foundation over the entire face, so as to drain all natural colour from the skin.

3 Using a 6mm (0.25 inch), flat-ended sable brush, start to apply shadows to the eye area, sinking the eye back into the socket as far as possible.

4 Continue to shadow the face, sinking in the temples and cheek hollows and thinning down the nose. Now add lines to the forehead, under the eyes and around the mouth.

5 The next stage is to break up the jawline with jowls and add shading to the neck and throat. With a clean 6mm (0.25 inch), flat-ended sable brush, add highlights to each of the shadows already applied, giving emphasis to all bony edges and heavy folds of flesh.

6 When the highlighting is finished, thoroughly powder the make-up with translucent powder.

7 If you need to suggest broken veins, they should be stippled on now with dark-red liner or lake, using a coarse stippling sponge.

8 Add wrinkles to the lips.

9 Replace the wig. Carefully fasten it into position with pins, grips and spirit gum.

10 Whiten the brows and lashes with white lining colour, using a small mascara brush.

Additional effects

When a rheumy-eyed effect is required, a thin line of a medium-red liner can be added to the inside edge of the lower lid. Gently pull the lid away from the eye with the tip of the little finger and then add the colour with a 3mm (0.125 inch), flat-ended, sable brush.

A tiny touch of the same red can be applied to the top lid to give a weak, sore look to the entire eye.

Where shading is insufficient to slim the nose effectively (on a very juvenile snub nose, for example) a thin aquiline effect can be obtained with the application of nose putty, before starting to apply your foundation.

These additional effects can be used for both men and women.

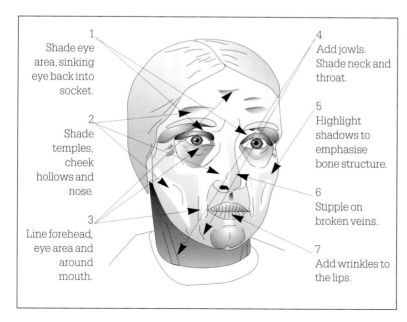

1
Shade eye area, sinking eye back into socket.

2
Shade temples, cheek hollows and nose.

3
Line forehead, eye area and around mouth.

4
Add jowls. Shade neck and throat.

5
Highlight shadows to emphasise bone structure.

6
Stipple on broken veins.

7
Add wrinkles to the lips.

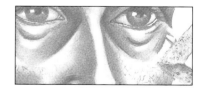

Broken veins and wrinkled lips add greatly to the aging effect

Thin old age

Thin old women

Follow the instructions on the previous page. Remember throughout that you must try to aim at a vertical treatment of the majority of the shadows and highlights.

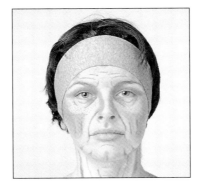

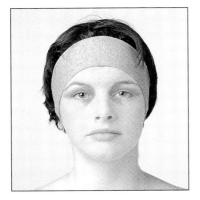

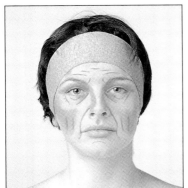

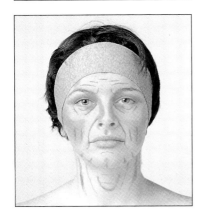

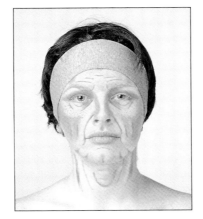

Colour guide

Foundation
For a pink and white complexion use pink groups mixed with white or pale groups. For sallow, ivory skin tones use ivory or sallow groups.

Shading
Olive-brown and lake groups

Highlights
White

Cheeks and lips
Dark-red or lake groups

Thin old men

The highlights and shadows are almost identical to those on the female chart. The only major differences are the balding wig, the thickening and coarsening of the eyebrows and, of course, the moustache.

Rounded old age

Rounded old age

Obesity and old age together present a number of make-up problems. first of all, a rounded face, for both men and women, will tend to look younger than a thin face, so it is very difficult for a young, thin actor or actress to be made to look both plump and old at the same time. Obviously, it is best to cast an actor who is already slightly overweight, or, at the very least, has a full, round face.

Also very young performers tend, unless they are extremely over-weight, not to have the necessary maturity to carry off the illusion of heaviness needed for this type of part.

There are two main optical illusions used to create the illusion of a stout face in the theatre. Horizontal detail will give maximum width to the fea-tures. Apply all your lines, wrinkles and folds of flesh in as horizontal a direction as possible. Wide hairstyles, beards and moustaches can also be used to increase the width of the face.

Make the eyes and mouth as small as possible. Then the rest of the face will appear bigger by way of contrast.

Rounded older women

The right hairstyle will help to suggest width. Choose a wig that is full at the sides and fairly flat on the top, with the hairline as far back as possible from the sides of the face. Try it on and check the general effect that it has on the shape of the face. Return it to the wig block.

1 First apply the foundation, which should be as light and bright as possible. Grease-based make-ups are best; they can be left slightly under-powdered to give the skin a suitably, shiny, hot look.

2 Apply moist rouge in a circle of colour on to the fullness of the cheek pads. Keep the strongest accent of colour around the outside of your circular pattern.

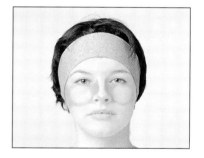

3 Use a warm, brown shading colour to shade the nose at the side and around the nostrils to give a small button-like appearance.

4 Apply shadows and lines to the eye area. Keep these as horizontal and wide as possible.

5 Add lines to the forehead, if neces-sary; keep these lines as long and horizontal as possible to add to the broadening effect.

6 Use shading colour to 'pull' the chin back into the throat. Paint on jowls and double chins with this.

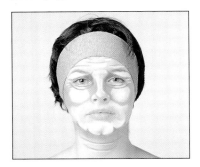

7 Highlight all the shadows. Pay particular attention to the fullness of the cheeks and the puffy areas around the eyes.

8 Paint on a small rounded mouth, highlighting the centre to give it a pouting appearance.

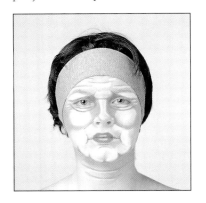

9 Add shadows and highlights to the corners of the mouth and to the flesh surrounding the lips to give as puffy an effect as possible.

Colour guide

Foundation:

For pink and white complexions use pale or pink groups mixed with florid groups.

For ruddy, florid complexions use sallow groups with florid and lake groups.

Shading:
Use olive-brown groups mixed with lake groups.

Highlights:
Use pale or ivory groups

Lips and cheeks:
Dark-red or lake groups

Eyeshadow:
Mauve tones

Rounded older men

Try on the chosen wig. Study the general effect on the shape of the face. A bald wig that has a hard dome, a wide forehead, and the hair puffed out at the sides and back will help the illusion of plumpness.

The best type has the dome built right down to the browbone with bushy eye-brows fastened along the edge. Now remove the wig to a wig block until the make-up is completed.

If you are using a false nose or nose putty, it should be applied now. An enlarged and coarsened nose helps this type of make-up enormously. If it is possible to make or obtain false double chins, they will contribute to the overall effect and should be applied at this stage.

1 Apply your foundation, mixing the colours with a stippling technique to give the complexion a really broken appearance.

2 Add rouge, stippling on until the foundation is built up. Emphasise the lower fullness of the cheek pad.

3 Using a 6mm (0.25 inch) sable brush, apply the shadows. These should be very red in tone. Keep all the shadows as horizontal as possible to give maximum width to the face.

Rounded old age

4 Apply highlights with a clean 6mm (0.25 inch) sable brush. Give maximum emphasis to the cheek pads, folds of the double chin and puffiness around the eyes.

5 Lightly powder make-up with translucent face powder.

6 Stipple on some broken veins, using lake lining colour on a coarse stippling sponge.

Colour guide

Foundation:
For highly florid complexions use pink stippled with florid and lake groups.

For sallow skins with florid overtones use ivory or sallow stippled with dark-red or lake groups.

Shading:
Lake mixed with olive-brown groups

Highlights:
Use ivory or pale groups.

Lips:
Use lake or dark-red groups.

7 Paint on a suitable, small, well-rounded mouth.

8 Intensify the shadow below the lower lip, using a very dark-brown pencil or lining colour. Highlight the centre of the mouth so as to give maximum fullness.

9 If the natural eyebrows are being used, whiten these with white lining colour or greasepaint on a mascara brush. Brush the colour on to

Ageing hands

It is very important to make up the hands if the character is old. The right highlighting and shading will emphasize the bone structure and give a skeletal appearance.

1 Ask the actor to make a fist so that the skin is stretched quite tightly. Apply circle of shadow over each knuckle.

2 Now press the outstretched fingers down on a flat surface. Apply highlight over the creases.

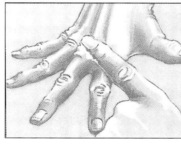

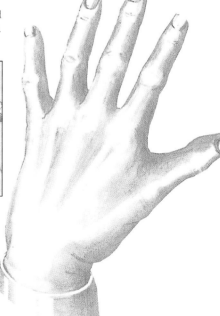

the brows in the opposite direction of the natural growth. Make them as fluffy and full as possible.

10 Replace the wig and fasten it securely in place with spirit gum and grips.

11 Make up hands with pink-toned body make-up. Redden the knuckles to give a suitable rounded puffy effect.

Additional effects

1 Some characters will benefit from a wide beard. Apply to the outer-most edge of the jawline to emphasise the fullness of the cheeks and the heaviness of the jowls.

2 Very full moustaches sweeping outwards and upwards under the cheek pads will give added fullness and add to the overall width of the face.

3 Where the natural brows are not strong, tease out white or grey crepe hair and used this to give a bushy effect. Extra face width can be suggested by exaggerating the full-ness at the outer ends of the brows.

3 Gently blend the edges of the highlights and shadows. A dust-ing of cake rouge will redden the knuckles, if this is needed.

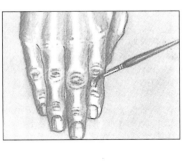

Raised veins can also be created with highlights and shadows. Use lining colours and pencils.

If the actor holds the hands in a claw-like position, with the thumbs and the little-finger tips tucked inside, this will add to the impression of age.

Small children

Very young children on a small stage may not need make-up at all. Much depends on the style of the show, on the characters being portrayed and the size of the auditorium. If the lights are powerful, then colour will be drained from their faces and so the aim is just to bring the colour levels back to normal, without their young faces looking 'artificial' and losing that natural innocent appeal.

1 Find a willing 'victim' who is sufficiently patient to be made up several times, if necessary.

2 Test the effect out front with no make-up at all.

3 Experiment with a very gentle make-up and then check the effect from out front again and adjust as necessary.

4 The eyes may benefit from some very subtle emphasis, even if no other make-up is needed.

5 Check the effect of natural colours of foundation with just a very little rouge and highlighting, if necessary.

6 Once the make-up level proves satisfactory for one child, then the other children can be made up to a similar degree.

If the children are playing character or animal roles, so that an exaggerated make-up is needed, there can be some excellent ideas and inspiration in the many books that are available now on face painting.

All young children can become rest-less and fidget if they are bored. It is important to involve them in the

Make up for girls

make-up process, explain what you are doing and why so that they will sit still long enough for you to complete the task comfortably.

In any event, plan the make-up beforehand and work as quickly as possible so that they are not subjected to a tedious over-long make-up routine and can enjoy the process.

Make-up for girls

Most young girls really enjoy the chance to wear make-up. Since this is normally 'forbidden territory' (trying out their mother's make-up is rarely encouraged) being given the opportunity to apply make-up has a special appeal. As with their adult counterparts, wearing make-up will add to their confidence and is part of the fun of the stage experience.

It can sometimes be quite a shock to the audience to see their offspring made up. If the roles are pseudo-adult (as in *Bugsy Malone*) this sudden sophistication and mature appearance can be quite unnerving – but very effective.

However, if the roles are straight children, then it is important to underplay the make-up so that the audience are unconscious of any artificiality.

Young, white skins are often quite fair, so choose a pale, straight female shade. The sort of natural colour that might be used for a 19th-century female effect works well.

Little girls look very appealing if the eyes are emphasised to look bigger

Girls with dark or black skins will need a cake make-up that will match their natural colour.

1 First apply a fine layer of cake foundation with a sponge.

2 Cover any spots with highlight. Powder well over these areas.

3 A little rouge can give a healthy look. Use a pink tone on white skins to match any natural warmth, and keep it soft; if you apply too much, then the child can look flushed and feverish.

4 Use a very pale cream stick make-up to highlight the eyelids. Blend it over the lids, and then powder.

5 Define the eyes with a line drawn along the lower eyelashes, using a brown pencil. Do not make this line too hard or too thick.

6 On medium to large stages, a shadow in the socket helps to define the top eyelid. Use a brown powder shadow for white skins and a charcoal one for black skins, working in the same way as you do for straight female make up. Unless the role is a sophisticated one, keep to soft, brown tones; blues and greens will look very false on a child.

7 Complete the eye make up with a little mascara. Unless the hair is naturally black, do not use black mascara. It is best not to use a waterproof mascara, either; its removal afterwards will be difficult.

Make-up for boys

8 Brush through the eyebrows to remove any make-up that may have been caught in the hairs. If the brows are quite dark, just apply a little clear grease (like Vaseline) or colour-free mascara – to give a shine.

9 If the brows need defining, work some powder shadow through them softly, in a colour to match the hair. This works better than pencil or cake for children because it gives soft definition without creating an unsuitably sophisticated shape. Alternatively, you can use block mascara for the eyelashes and the eyebrows.

10 A bright red lipstick on little girls' lips is far too harsh. It will make them look doll-like, as well as emphasising the smallness of the natural mouth. Use a soft peach instead – or a pink, so long as it is not too garish.

Make-up for boys

While young girls are only too eager to experiment with make-up, boys may well resist the idea. It is certainly not the 'macho' thing to do and it is especially important to keep the make-up very light and discreet. Most young lads will be highly embarrassed by any make-up that looks effeminate or overdone.

As with young children, if you can use the stage and lighting beforehand it is very helpful to see how the natural, unadorned skin looks under the lights from the auditorium before deciding how to proceed.

If the boy's role is a very minor one and the make-up team's resources are already overstretched, you may be able to avoid using any make-up at all. Generally, however, the strength of the lights will drain the skin colour and some small amount of make-up will be needed to redress this. Especially if making up boys is a new experience, it is useful to test out various degrees of make-up under the lights until the right natural effect is achieved.

Be careful not to use too dark a colour on white skins. There is sometimes a tendency to think that boys need darker base make-up than girls. This is not so. Boys' and girls' skin tones are much the same. A straight female foundation is usually a good choice. Hispanic and dark skins, of course, will need a matching foundation.

1 Apply a thin wash of cake or creamy foundation and pat dry with a tissue.

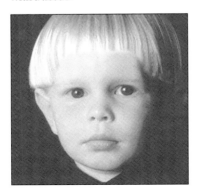

2 If the performance is in a medium or large theatre, emphasise the eyes by placing a dot of pale highlight on each eyelid.

3 Blend the highlight quickly over the lids, then powder it.

4 If you have chosen a creamy cake it might be wise to powder the whole face at this point.

5 Very fair eyelashes and eyebrows can be darkened with a little block mascara.

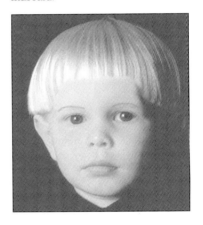

If the face needs more colour, use a little dry rouge in the male position. On boys' skins that are pale, use the usual colour for women; darker skins will need a stronger colour.

Make-up en masse for children

Make-up en masse for children

Often the children will be performing in a school production, a pantomime, ballet or dance show that involves exotic characters rather than 'natural' children. Many of these effects will be explored later in *Special Shows and Styles* and *Exciting Characters* (pages 116-151).

However, it must be admitted that if dealing with children en masse certain short-cuts may need to be taken, and the make-up expertise is likely to be considerably thinned if very large numbers of young actors are involved.

It is more important than ever to be well organised and to allocate work loads appropriately, leaving the most skilled work to the experts and basic foundation work to a team of less skilled helpers. The section on *Make-up en masse* in section 2 *Organisation*

makes suggestions about organising make-up for large numbers.

If dealing with many small children it is even more vital to be well prepared and to have organised a well-structured plan of campaign. Otherwise, chaos will reign!

Face paint and fantasy roles

There may well be a team of people in your area who have experimented with face paint at parties and social events. While this is not recommended for straight make-up in a conventional production, if there are many fantasy roles in a show that is pure escapism and the numbers of artistes needing make-up seems daunting, then it may be appropriate to seek the help of experienced face painters or for the existing make-up team to practice the skills of using face paint rather than stage make-up.

Using face paint has several advantages:

1
It is fast and easy to apply.

2
It washes off rather more easily than conventional stage paint, so is ideal for small children, and is less likely to cause allergic reactions than heavier stage make-up (although there are exceptions to this).

3
Specialised application skills are less essential.

Disadvantages are:

1
It does not look natural so is applicable only for fantasy roles.

2
The make-up is rather 'flat' but can be combined with special effects such as 'Derma' wax, false hair and artificial blood to achieve fun special effects and attain a three-dimensional quality. Use fake blood with great care as it can stain clothing.

The kit

Face paints come in single pots or in a palette.

The make-up is generally applied with make-up sponges.

Detailed work will need a range of brushes; or at the very least one thick and one fine brush for each artiste.

Always check the effect from 'out front' and make sure the style of all the individual make-ups is co-ordinated

Face paint and fantasy roles

Face painting techniques

1 Rub a wet, well-squeezed-out sponge lightly in the paint.

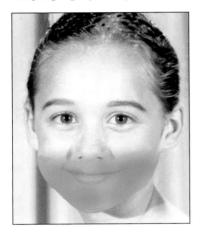

2 Dab the sponge over the face until the face paint is evenly applied, not forgetting the chin line, eyelids and nose creases.

3 Keep dabbing and gently pushing the sponge. Never try to drag it across the face in long strokes.

4 Make sure the paint has been taken right up to the hairline and into all the facial creases.

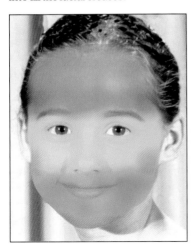

5 Now apply details with a brush. Keep this brush at right angles to the face.

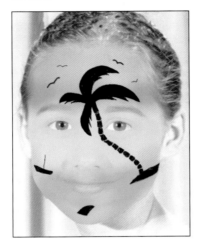

6 Lay the bristles flat to make a thicker line.

7 Use the tip of the brush to make a fine line or a dot.

This is an extravagant Hawaiian beach design, but the possibilities with face painting designs are endless; they can be as subtle or wild as the play theme or character demands

Face paint tips

1

Face paint can be combined very effectively with conventional make-up. For example, ordinary lipstick or stage lip colour will last much longer than face paint on the lips so use this in preference. Make up blusher can also be applied over face paint.

2

In general, it is best to add details by working from the top of the face downwards. However, for practical reasons, once the brush or sponge is 'loaded' it is sensible to do all the details in a particular colour before reloading the brush with a fresh shade.

3

A stipple sponge is useful for certain effects. It is made of coarse mesh. Wet it, squeeze it, and then rub it in the paint. Dab it gently on the face to create a speckled effect. Stubbly chins, snowflakes, stars, hazy effects, speckles and so on can be achieved. Experiment to see what works best to suit the roles involved in a particular production.

4

Special effects 'Derma wax' and nose putty can be used to create three-dimensional effects. A whole variety of nose shapes, wounds or lumps can then painted over with face paint that is dabbed over the wax with a sponge. There are more details on using wax in the special effects section. Certainly this is an ideal way to create boils, warts, scars and wounds that may be applicable to witches, monsters, pirates and other fantasy characters that are likely to be portrayed by children.

5

Artificial noses, ears and eyes can be bought from make-up suppliers or from joke shops.

Face paint and fantasy roles

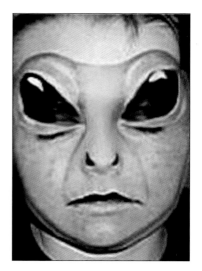

General notes on making up children

Making up children does not require any very different skills from making up adult actors but the following need to be borne in mind:

1 Most children will really enjoy the

experience of being changed and made to look different but they can become very excited and need to be well controlled.

2 Children's patience and ability to sit still will be limited if the process is too prolonged so experiment and plan the make-up thoroughly first – and then

find ways to complete the process as simply and quickly as possible.

3 A good working team will need to be organised well in advance if relatively large numbers of children need to be made up at the same time. Very young children, especially, should not be made up too far in advance of the per-

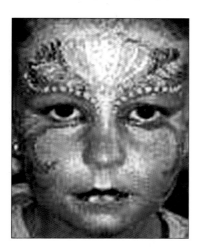

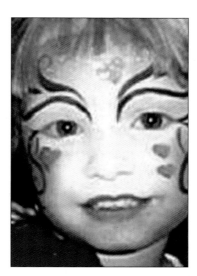

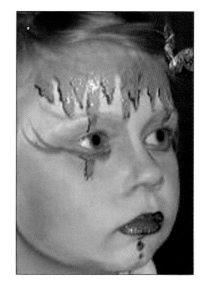

Face paint and fantasy roles

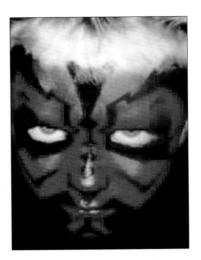

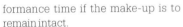

formance time if the make-up is to remain intact.

4 Children's young skins can be sensitive and certainly they should be supervised to make sure all the make-up is properly removed at the end of the show.

To sum up

This section has looked at the 'who and how' of relatively conventional make-up. Succeeding chapters will examine special effects and how to create more exotic characters, whether from other parts of the world or from the realms of fantasy.

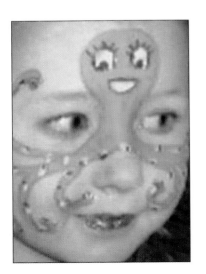

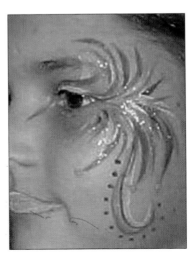

Wigs, beards and special effects

More than make-up

Making up the face with appropriate conventional make-up will generally turn out to be the main responsibility of the make-up artist. However, there are lots of other fascinating areas that are also controlled by the make-up team. These include the dressing and use of hair and wigs, the application of false pieces such as beards and noses, and the creation of special effects like scars and tattoos.

Generally a great deal of fun can be had in learning how to build the actor or actress into a very different character through these various means.

Hair, wigs and colour effects

Greying and colouring the hair

The simplest method of greying the hair is with white cornstarch powder but this gives the hair a lifeless appearance. Moreover, the powder is very easily displaced.

Whitener applied with a tinting brush is much better.

However, this method can be long and tedious when greying a full head of hair and the hair is subsequently quite difficult to style. It may well be easier to use hair colour. They come in a wide variety of colours, including silver, white and grey.

Hair colour sprays
Cut a template to match the hairline and then use this to mask the face as you spray the front sections of hair. Be careful not make the greying look too white or it will appear blue and slightly artificial when it is seen under the stage lighting.

Hair colour streaks

1 To create a streak in the hair, take a sheet of foolscap parchment paper and cut a slit about 50mm/2 inches long in the middle.

2 Pull a lock of hair through this hole and press the paper as close to the scalp as possible.

3 Spread the lock of hair over the paper and then spray with the chosen colour. Allow it to dry, remove the paper and comb the lock back into the hair.

Greasepaint or cream-stick make-up is particularly effective for small localised applications such as at the temples or for streaks, but can rub off.

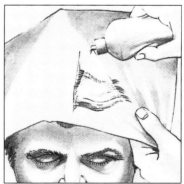

Apart from greying the hair, sprays can be used to change the hair to almost any colour.

Also, hair can be professionally lightened and then given a temporary colour rinse to suit the role.

Hairpieces

Wigs cover natural hair completely, while hairpieces just supplement the natural growth. Hairpieces must blend into the natural hair, so when ordering from a wigmaker, enclose a snippet of the actor's own hair to ensure a true match.

Switches and chignons

These are the easiest hairpieces to use. They are simply pinned into position without having to be blended into the natural hair.

Adding a switch to lengthen hair

Falls

These sections of hair can be used by both men and women. They are especially useful for period styles when loose flowing hair is needed at the back of the head. Part the hair across the top of the head from ear to ear and securely pin the fall along the parting and into the back hair. The hair in front of the parting is then combed back over the edge of the fall and into the false hair. It is pinned in place with fine hairpins.

This is often more effective than using a full wig, since the front hairline is natural and there is no wig join to conceal. It is also likely to be preferred by the actor, rather than a full wig, as it is not so hot and itchy and can be worn for a long period without discomfort.

A hairpiece or 'fall' pinned at the back

Curls

Curls are very simple to use. They can be fixed in a number of ways, either pinned under the natural curls or loops of hair, tied into place with ribbons or simply fastened underneath bonnets or head-dresses.

Toupees

These are used to disguise a receding hairline. Good toupees have a fine hair-lace front, are expensive and need to be treated carefully. Less expensive toupees do not have lace fronts, are much stronger and easier to apply. Unfortunately, these cheaper toupees can look very false, unless the front hair can be dressed forward in a fringe to hide the hairline.

Wigs

Generally these are hired or purchased from a theatrical wigmaker but there are also many very good women's wigs, made from artificial hair, on sale in beauty parlours, hairdressers and departmental stores.

Hard edge wig

This type has a so-called 'hard edge'; the hair is knotted directly to the front of the wig foundation and does not have a natural-looking hairline.

1 Dress the wig hair forward into a fringe or a set of curls so the hard edge is concealed or comb forward a narrow section of your own hair over the face, along the natural hairline.

2 Put on the wig with the hard edge along this parting.and fasten the wig in place with hairpins or grips.

3 Brush the natural hair back over wig until the two blend together.

A 'Cleopatra' wig

Lace front wig

This type of wig is similar to a toupee, which is stuck to the forehead with spirit gum.

Wigs

Blender

This type of wig has a blender, which is made of tightly woven gauze stretched across the forehead. This blender must be covered with make-up so that it matches the rest of the face. These wigs are particularly useful if the character requires a bald head or a very high forehead.

Putting on a lace-front wig

Before putting on a wig, the natural hair must be flattened to the head as much as possible. Men with short hair may not need to do this, but if a very heavy periwig is being worn, a strip of bandage wound twice around the head provides a base to which the wig can be firmly pinned in position.

1 Short and medium-length hair should be pinned in small circular curls, flat to the scalp, evenly all over.

2 Long hair should be divided right down the centre and wound around the head, folding the two sections over each other at the back and firmly pinning them in place.

3 Cover the flattened hair with a cotton gauze or crepe bandage, or with the top of an old stocking made into a cap.

4 Grasp the wig by the two springs at the back edge and carefully position front join so it is touching the centre of the forehead. Pull wig firmly but gently backwards with both hands, until the springs are nestling comfortably into the nape of the neck.

5 Now place and adjust its position. Gently ease it back until the join is exactly where it is required.

6 Take hold of the springs at each side of the wig and pull them gently into position (so that they are just in front of the ears). Pin them securely to the bandage.

7 Fasten the two net side-flaps to the skin with spirit gum, pressing them firmly into place with a damp towel. Gum the centre of the join to the forehead in order to prevent the wig riding up. If the join does not seem tight enough, fasten it with spirit gum around the hairline.

Putting on a blender front

When using a blender front, it is first necessary to cover the gauze with appropriate make-up to match the colour on your face.

1 Apply foundation colour to the face. Carry the colour on to the forehead, well above the line where the join of the wig will be. Thoroughly powder the forehead.

2 Put on the wig. Use a piece of thin tissue or greaseproof wrapping-paper between the blender and the actor's hair in order to prevent the make-up sinking through the gauze into the hair.

3 Make up the gauze front or bald top with a greasepaint foundation. Adjust the colour so that it matches the make-up on the forehead. Do any character work that is needed. Now thoroughly powder the front until the greasepaint is set. Carefully remove the wig, lift away protective paper, and powder the inside of the blender which will still be greasy.

Wigs

4 It should only be repainted about once a week or when it becomes discoloured. It is a good idea to remove some of the first application of greasepaint with surgical spirit or acetone before renewing the make-up so that the build-up is kept to a minimum.

Putting on a toupee

Take care that the toupee sits where the natural hairline would be, or even slightly higher.

1 If the toupee has a lace front, place it in position and brush a thin coat of spirit gum on to the dry skin, devoid of any make-up, immediately below the lace.

2 Allow spirit gum to dry slightly. Press the lace front into position, using a dampened, lintless towel.

3 The back of the toupee must now be fastened in place, using either double-sided toupee tape directly on to the scalp or by pinning the toupee to the back hair with a grip sewn on to the back edge of the foundation.

Hard-fronted toupees should be attached with toupee tape both at the front and back.

Dressing and caring for wigs

Once unpacked, the wig should be kept on a wig block so that it does not lose its shape and can be easily redressed. If you do not have a wig block, the wig should be returned to its box or itcan be kept on an inexpensive styrofoam head form.

How to dress a wig

1 Pin the wig to the wig block with wig pins.

2 Brush and comb it out thoroughly. Do not let the comb dig into the foundation.

Wig measurements

1
Circumference of the head average 560mm (22 inches)

2
Front hairline to nape of neck average 355mm (14 inches)

3
Ear to ear across forehead

4
From ear to ear over the top of the head average 305mm (12 inches)

5
Temple to temple round back of head average 405mm (16 inches)

Beard measurements

A
Sideburn to sideburn under the chin

B
Lip to end of beardline under the chin

C
Round the front to back of jawbone

Wigs

3 For a softly-waved style, simply curl with an electric curling tong.

4 If a stronger wave is required, put the hair up into pin curls or on rollers, first moistening each section of hair by spraying it with water or hair-setting lotion. The curls or rollers should be placed in the direction in which the hair is to be combed out when dry.

5 Cover the wig with a net and dry thoroughly with a hairdryer.

6 Remove all rollers and pins, brush out the hair and style as required.

7 Spray with light hairspray.

Removing wigs and toupees

Apply spirit-gum solvent with a brush to the gummed areas until the lace begins to lift. Then, with both hands, grasp the foundation at the back of the wig or toupee and pull it gently forward and off.

When removing a wig with a blender front, work some spirit-gum solvent underneath one end of the blender edge with a flat brush and gradually ease the brush along under the edge as the solvent dissolves the gum. Then remove the wig.

Cleaning wigs and toupees

Immediately after removing a wig or toupee, clean the spirit gum off the join with acetone or carbon tetrachloride. Do not use cotton balls because the fibres stick to the lace. Under no circumstances ever attempt to use shampoo on a wig.

If possible, store the wig on a proper wig stand.

Beards and moustaches

The most realistic false beards, moustaches and side whiskers are those knotted on to fine hair or nylon lace. These are obtainable from wigmakers or good stage suppliers. They should always be applied with spirit gum (not latex, which would ruin the hair lace).

Do not clean off the foundation where you are going to apply a beard or moustache; it is better to leave a fine film of well-powdered foundation on the skin; this acts as a barrier to the spirit gum, making it more comfortable to apply.

Usually when you receive a beard, a moustache or side-whiskers from a wigmaker, you will find a very wide margin of hair lace around the actual shape of the piece. This must be carefully trimmed. Do this in a good light so you can see the very fine knots of fairer hair at the hairline. You need to trim the lace about two or three holes away from the actual hairline.

Once the piece has been trimmed, apply as follows:

Removing and cleaning a hairpiece

To remove a hairpiece woven on to a lace foundation, moisten the lace with spirit-gum solvent until the gum is dissolved. The piece can then be gently peeled away.

The edge of the lace should then be thoroughly cleaned with acetone so that it is ready to be used again.

Between performances, these pieces should be stored in the wigmaker's boxes so they do not become flattened or the lace damaged.

Attaching a nylon-lace beard

1 Place the beard piece on the face, exactly where it needs to be stuck, and note the area covered by the lace so that you can determine where to apply the spirit gum.

2 Brush a thin film of spirit gum exactly where the lace will go. Allow it to dry completely. Lightly load brush with spirit gum and remoisten the gummed area.

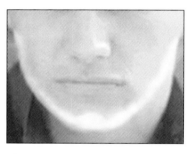

3 Make sure your hands are clean. Place the hairpiece carefully in position. Press the edges firmly on to the face with the dampened corner of a linen towel.

4 Where a beard or side-whiskers meet the natural sideburns, lift the bottom edge of the sideburns with a comb and stick the lace under the growth of hair. Then comb the natural

Beards and moustaches

hair into the false hair until they blend together. If there still is a gap between the false beard and the natural growth, fill this in with a small amount of crepe hair – or add a few strokes of matching eyebrow pencil.

Using crepe hair

Well-made hair-lace pieces are quite expensive to buy and, because of their fragile nature, are not hired out by wigmakers.

If your budget does not allow you to purchase these, then you must learn to use wool-crepe hair. This is relatively inexpensive but must be applied with skill if it is to look natural. Solid colours do not look natural so always buy crepe hair with mixed colours in the braid. The only exceptions are black hair for a black make-up or primary colours for a stylised make-up.

When using crepe hair to make beards and moustaches, as well as spirit gum and solvent, you will need the following:

1
a small pair of very sharp hairdressing or moustache scissors

2
a small lintless towel

3
a selection of crepe hair in different colours

Preparation of wool crepe

1 Crepe hair is supplied in tight braids bound with string and needs straightening before use. Undo the string and cut off a piece that mea-sures about 150mm (6 inches) long when stretched out.

2 Holding both ends of the piece, immerse it in a bowl of warm water and move it gently around until it begins to lose its strong curl.

3 Now tease it out a little, still float-ing it on the surface of the water.

4 Lift the 'mat' of hair out of the water. Lay it on a piece of towel or on kitchen paper.

5 Repeat this process until you have sufficient mats of hair for your par-ticular needs.

6 You must now allow the mats of hair to dry completely

7 Store the mats of hair between the pages of an old book, secured with a rubber band.

Making a chin beard

1 Divide a mat of crepe hair, cutting off the two ends 1 and 6

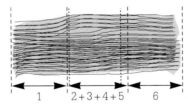

2 Divide the middle section into four equal pieces with your fingers. Separate each section into the shapes as shown.

3 Paint the entire area of the chin to be bearded with the spirit gum lightly loaded on a brush. Allow chin to dry completely.

4 Remoisten the underpart of the chin with a lightly loaded brush. Lay section 1 in place, with the hair coming forward from the top of the throat to the point of the chin. Press this carefully and firmly in place with a moistened towel.

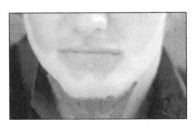

5 Remoisten the sides of the jaw just above section 1. Lay sections 2 and 3 in place, parallel to and touching section 1. Press into place with the moistened towel.

Beards and moustaches

6 Remoisten the areas just above sections 2 and 3, along the top of the jawbone and rising towards the corners of the mouth. Lay sections 4 and 5 in place, touching 2 and 3. Press these into position.

7 Remoisten front of chin and lay section 6 in place. Keep the centre point just below the centre of lower lip and the two outside points joining sections 4 and 5 at the corners of the mouth. Press into place with a moistened towel.

8 Now allow all the sections to dry completely.

9 Gently stroke the beard with your fingers, blending all the sections together and also removing any stray loose hairs.

10 Trim and shape beard with sharp hairdressing scissors to the required style.

11 For a full facial beard, simply continue this process up the side of the face as far as the sideburn, with short sections of hair overlapping like roof tiles.

Stubble beards

A four-day-old stubble beard can be simulated by using crepe hair.

1 Pull a length of crepe hair out of the braid and snip it into pieces approximately 6mm (0.25 inch) in length. Store these clippings in a small box.

2 Apply a thin film of spirit gum over the beard and moustache area and allow to become tacky.

3 Pick up a ball of the hair clippings with your fingertips and pull it in half. Dab the clippings on to the gummed face. Start by the side-burns

on each side of the face and use both hands. Avoid getting gum on the fingertips.

4 After about six dabs, pick up a new ball of clippings and continue the process, working down the sides of the face.

5 Continue on to the top lip, on to the chin and down the throat until the required density of stubble has been applied.

6 If the gum becomes too dry for hair to adhere, stop at once and remoisten it.

Beards and moustaches

A simple wool-crepe moustache

1 Apply a thin coat of spirit gum to the entire top lip and allow to dry.

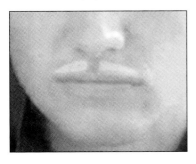

2 From a mat of crepe hair, cut three straight sections that measure approximately 12mm (0.5 inch), 18mm (0.75 inch) and 25mm (1 inch).

3 Remoisten a thin line of the gum just above the mouth. Hold the 12mm (0.5 inch) section of hair between your first fingers and thumbs. Gently pull down with your thumbs and push up with your fingers so that the straight cut becomes bevelled and all the hair-ends are visible.

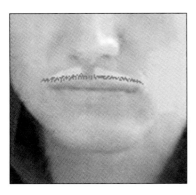

4 Lay this strip of hair along the moistened edge of the lip, slightly twisting the hair outwards. Then press it in place with the moistened corner of your towel.

5 Remoisten the gum just above the first section. Make sure that the gum goes over the ends of the first layer of hair.

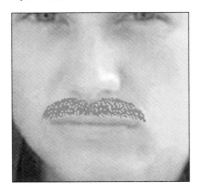

6 Lay the 12mm (0.5 inch) section of hair in place. Bevel the edge as before and twist hair outwards again. Press into place with a damp towel.

7 Remoisten remaining gummed area, once more allowing gum to cover the ends of the previous section. This area will be divided in two by the centre wing of the nostrils.

8 Take the last section, bevel as before, and then separate it into two halves.

9 Apply each half to either side of the lip, turning the hair well outwards to simulate natural growth. Press the hair into place with a dampened towel.

10 Allow to dry completely and tease out any loose hairs with thumb and forefinger.

11 Trim along the base of the moustache with hairdressing scissors and remove any long hairs that might irritate the nose.

A longer wool-crepe moustache

1 First cut off the end of the mat of hair, at 35-50mm (almost 2 inch) – depending on how long the moustache is to be.

2 Divide this section lengthways into four.

3 Take two pieces and pull them between finger and thumb until the wide end of the section is bevelled. Twist the thin end into a point.

Beards and moustaches

4 Following the same gumming and pressing technique as above, apply these two shaped sections as shown. The remaining two pieces can be used for your next moustache.

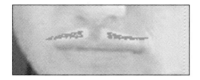

5 Now overlay short sections of hair over the centre area, angling them so that they flow in the direction of growth of the two side-pieces.

6 Gum and press as before.

Mutton-chop whiskers

1 These can be simulated with unstraightened crepe, pulled directly from the braid and moulded with fingers.

2 Attach the fluffy sections along the jawline, double gumming but not pressing the hair too firmly with your towel.

3 Now add small sections of hair up to the natural side-burns, overlapping like tiles as in the full facial beard.

Remember when working with crepe hair to keep your fingers and scissors absolutely clean and free from spirit gum by wiping them with solvent as you proceed.

Bald heads

Bald caps should be well matched to the facial colour if they are to look natural. Made from latex, they adapt to the shape of the head to fit snugly. Paper-thin ones work best. The cap should be large enough to cover the ears. Glue the main part of the cap into position and trim to fit. Roll back the edges to glue them, stretch out wrinkles and then stick the edges down firmly. Dab on a thin layer of liquid latex to overlap the edge. Once this is dry, coat the film with sealer before making up.

Alternatively, you can create a bald pate by soaping down the real hair. Cover the head with a nylon stocking, soap again, paint with cream stick and then powder.

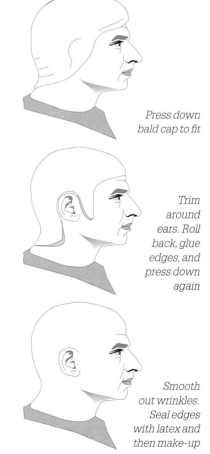

Press down bald cap to fit

Trim around ears. Roll back, glue edges, and press down again

Smooth out wrinkles. Seal edges with latex and then make-up

Three-dimensional make-up

Three-dimensional make-up

A great many changes can be made to an actor's face simply by modelling it with light and shade, but these changes are optical illusions. They do not actually change the physical outlines of the face.

Sometimes this is not completely convincing, particularly with features such as the nose or chin – especially in profile. It may be necessary to make physical changes with false pieces, pre-made in rubber latex or plastic. Alternatively, you can use nose putty or DermaWax.

False pieces

The most satisfactory method of building up the features is by using false pieces. These must be well made and fit the actor's face if they are to be convincing.

False latex pieces should be stuck into place before any make-up has been applied to the skin. Spirit gum or latex adhesive can be used for this, but since latex adhesive can be more easily loosened by perspiration and muscular movement under the piece, spirit gum is the better choice.

Noses are the most usual false pieces to be used, but the method of application remains the same for other pieces – eye pouches, chins, and so on.

Applying false pieces: noses

1 Place the piece in position on the nose to check the fit. Note how much excess latex is around the edge of the piece.

2 Trim away this excess edging with very sharp scissors, keeping the outline as irregular as possible because straight edges are harder to camouflage.

3 Apply a thin film of spirit gum about 12mm (0.5 inch) wide along the inside edge of the piece.

4 Allow the gum to become tacky before placing the false piece on the skin. Place the false nose very carefully in the exact position required. Do not adjust the position once it is in place, as this wrinkles the edges and will make them more difficult to conceal.

5 Using a dampened lintless towel wrapped around your fingertip, press the edges of the false nose into place. The crease at the back of the nostrils can be pressed in place using the blunt end of an orange-(or hoof-) stick or similar manicure tool.

6 If the edges of the piece are thick, they can be concealed with a small amount of liquid latex adhesive stippled along the join. This must be allowed to dry completely before applying make-up to the piece.

Making up false pieces

As greasepaint tends to make rubber latex deteriorate, it is best to make-up false pieces with a special rubber-mask greasepaint based on castor oil.

This can prove to be quite expensive – especially as it is often necessary to use two or three different shades of paint to camouflage a false piece.

False pieces: advantages

There are many advantages of such pre-made pieces:

They are quick and easy to apply and remove.

They always give a constant shape.

Generally they are light and comfortable to wear.

They usually stay firmly in place.

They are not very susceptible to damage, so the actor wears them with confidence.

They can be used for such things as eye pouches, double chins, sagging throats, false eyelids, and so on – items which cannot be made from putty and wax.

False pieces: disadvantages

False pieces have two main disadvantages:

Firstly, they are expensive to buy.

Secondly, they are difficult to obtain. Ideally, they ought to be made-to-measure and this means a visit to a specialist in this field.

Of course it is possible to make them for yourself but this can be very time-consuming and complicated. For those who wish to try, there are a number of excellent books on the subject. (See the *Further Reading* section on page 153.)

Three-dimensional make-up

If this proves too much for your budget, a good substitute is cream-based stick make-up, applied with a little castor oil.

1 First apply your chosen base to the rest of the face, stopping just short of the edge of your applied false piece.

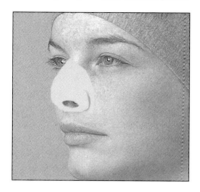

2 With your fingertip, work a small amount of castor oil over the top of the stick make-up until it is well mixed. Stipple the mixture over the false piece, carefully blending the colour into the foundation you have already applied.

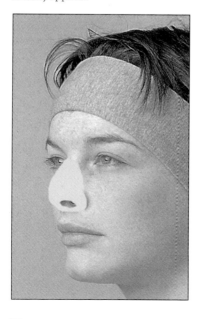

3 Powder well.

4 Check the colour difference between the make-up on the false piece and on the skin. Adjust by stippling on darker and lighter shades of your original base colour with a stippling sponge.

5 Powder again.

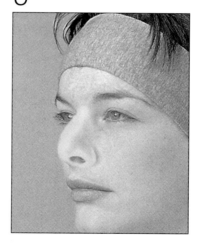

It is sometimes necessary to add a little rouge to features such as the nose or ears. This can be done by stippling on cream rouge when you adjust the colour to the skin.

Alternatively, apply cake rouge with a rouge mop, after powdering. Do this very carefully. Gradually build up the depth of colour required, as it is very difficult to remove.

Nose putty

Sometimes false pieces are too expensive for the budget – or difficult to obtain.

If you do not have the time or skill to manufacture your own false pieces, then nose putty or Derma Wax can be used to good effect.

Both these 'builds' require a certain amount of expertise. If using them for the first time, don't leave it too late to practise before the opening night.

Nose putty is generally used to build up and change the shape of the nose, but it can be used for other features as well, providing that they have a firm bony base and are not subject to a lot of muscular movement which would dislodge the putty.

You will be surprised how little putty is needed to make quite startling changes to the shape of the nose, and it is a good idea to practise with small quantities of putty before embarking on really big builds.

1 Before starting to build up the nose, decide on the shape you want. Find a picture or make a profile sketch of the shape required. Tape this reference to the make-up mirror.

2 Make sure that the area to which you are applying the putty is clean and free from grease. Cleanse the skin beforehand with a little toning lotion on a cotton ball.

3 Now apply the putty. Take a small piece of putty from the stick and gently knead it with the fingertips until it is pliable. If the putty sticks to

the fingertips, rub a fine film of hair-dressing gel over the fingertips before continuing the application.

4 Press the ball of putty on the part of the nose to be built up.

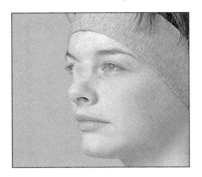

5 Gently start to press the nose putty down at the sides, using the first finger and thumb.

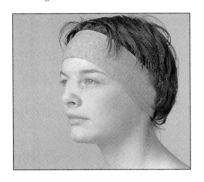

6 Continue to blend and shape the nose in this way, thinning the edges of the putty into the skin.

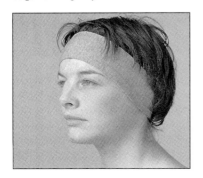

7 Once the edges of the nose putty are blended into the skin, adjust the shape by squeezing and pressing the putty until it resembles the required outline.

8 Put some make-up base on to a fingertip and gently stipple the colour on to the putty nose, carefully massaging the surface to smooth out any unwanted bumps or cracks.

9 Gently powder nose. Now apply the make-up to the rest of the face.

The putty is generally lighter than the natural skin colour and it is usually necessary to adjust the colouring on the build by stippling on a deeper shade of your chosen base colour.

If you accidentally knock or rub the surface of the nose during the performance, the make-up can be disturbed and the underlying pale putty shows through. Avoid this by adding a small amount of a very dark cream-stick make-up to the putty when you first knead it, changing its colour to something nearer the natural skin tone.

Removing a putty nose

Hold the build between your finger and thumb and gently rock the putty until it works loose. Lift the nose away and squeeze it into a ball – which you can then use to lift away any remaining pieces of putty left around the edges of the build. Any small fragments that remain can be massaged with removing cream and wiped off with a facial tissue.

The putty ball can be kept and re-used a number of times, although eventually the successive addition of make-up base will make it too sticky and pliable to use easily.

Derma Wax

Derma Wax has a much softer texture than nose putty. It can be moulded and shaped more easily. It is, however, more susceptible to damage if accidentally knocked and needs to have a protective film of sealer painted over it before the make-up is applied. Perspiration, or a small amount of muscular movement at the sides of the build, can easily dislodge this protective film. However, its indetectability, even close-up, makes Derma Wax invaluable for film or photographic make-up or for drama in the round or intimate theatres.

To prevent wax being easily dislodged with perspiration, it is necessary to create a 'key' (a base which aids adhesion) before starting the build. This is done as follows:

1 Paint the area of the build with spirit gum and apply a thin layer of cotton (cotton wool) over gummed area. Press gently into place and allow to dry.

Three-dimensional make-up

2 Pull off excess cotton, to leave a slightly fluffy surface over the build area. This will provide a key to which the wax will adhere.

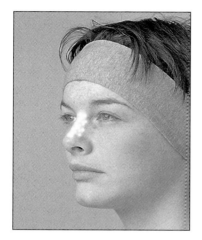

3 Knead a small amount of very dark, cream-stick foundation into a lump of Derma Wax. (Use a palette knife on a plastic palette, rather than fingers, which can make the wax too warm and soft.)

4 Carry on until the wax is much the same colour as the natural skin tone; then roll the wax into a ball and press it on to the fluffy key.

5 Gently blend and shape the wax into the shape required. Do not apply cream or gel to the fingers but dip them in cold water to prevent the wax adhering to them.

6 There may still be a tendency for the wax to pull away. Use the handle of a teaspoon, dipped in cold water, as a spatula to mould the wax.

7 Paint a fine film of sealer over the entire build, using a flat-ended, soft bristle brush. Use a cheap brush as the sealer and solvent used for cleaning will soon ruin a good sable brush. Once the sealer is completely dry, the build can be made up as described before.

Removal of Derma Wax

If you do not wish to re-use the wax, the build can simply be removed by pulling it away with a tissue.

If you wish to retain the wax for further use, the sealer must first be carefully lifted and peeled away from the wax, before it is removed. Final traces of wax and sealer should be massaged with make-up cleanser and wiped away with a tissue.

Creating a wrinkled skin

Physically wrinkling the skin will achieve a really old look. But, however effective a finely wrinkled surface on the skin may look in the mirror or when seen on film or television, under stage lighting and viewed from a distance, it will become almost invisible.

There are techniques that can be used to wrinkle the skin coarsely enough for it to show in the theatre, but it needs a good deal of patience and skill to make this wrinkling look natural. Often the result looks more like a horror mask than graceful old age. However, for those who wish to try it, here is the simplest method of wrinkling – applying cleansing tissue over liquid latex or spirit gum.

1 Tear a single thickness of facial cleansing tissue into sections to cover the right shape and area of skin. (Do not be tempted to use very large sections as they quickly become unmanageable.) Use peach or brown coloured tissue to achieve the most natural results.

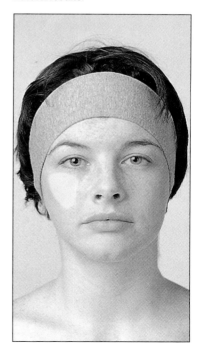

Three-dimensional make-up

2 Stretch a small area of skin taut between the first finger and the thumb. Now paint it with a fine film of liquid latex or spirit gum.

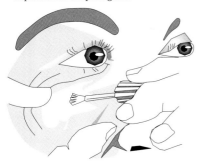

3 When the gummed area has become slightly tacky, apply a section of the torn tissue to the area. Then

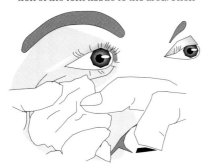

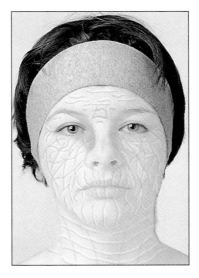

apply a second coat of latex or gum over the surface of the tissue.

4 With the skin still stretched taut, dry the area with a hairdryer.

5 Release the skin and note how the skin will wrinkle.

6 Repeat the process on adjacent areas of skin.

7 Once the whole face has been covered with the gummed tissue and has completely dried, it can be made up with grease or cream-stick stippled over the surface.

8 Using a shade lighter than the colour of the gummed tissue, highlight just the tops of the wrinkles for emphasis.

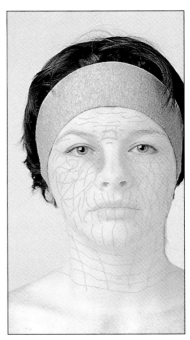

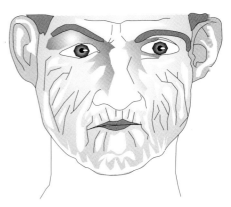

If latex and tissue has been used, the wrinkled skin can very simply be peeled away from the face, but if spirit gum is used then use a spirit gum solvent to soften the application before its removal.

Special effects

Nose plugs

Nostrils can be enlarged and coars-ened by the insertion of nose plugs. These can be made from small plastic thimbles (each with a hole drilled through the top) or small plastic cur-tain rings. The most effective, and the most comfortable to wear, are made from the tip of a baby's pacifier or a section of soft teat (nipple) from a baby's feeding bottle.

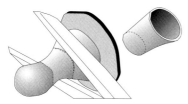

1 Cut a section from the middle of the teat (nipple). (The actual size will vary according to the size of the performer's nostril and how much you wish to enlarge it.)

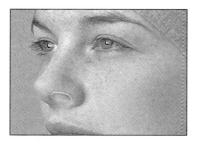

2 Insert the plug by placing it on the tip of your little finger and gently inserting it into the nostril.

3 Conceal inside of plug and visible edge with make-up.

When using a baby's pacifier, make a hole in the tip, cut off the top of the bulb and then proceed as before. Remember to make the hole in the tip or the actor will have some difficulty breathing!

Wounds and scars

Scars can be suggested with the use of greasepaint but to be fully effective they need to be three-dimensional. The simplest method is to use non-flexible collodion.

1 Paint the area to be scarred with collodion and allow it to dry.

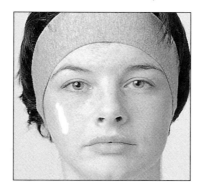

2 As it dries, it contracts and puck-ers the skin.

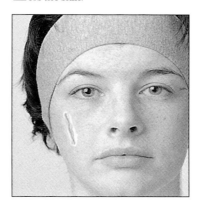

3 If the effect is not deep enough, apply a number of successive coats, allowing each application to dry completely before applying the next layer.

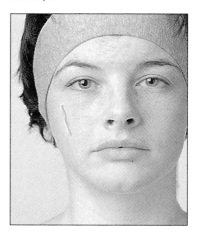

4 This indented scar can be further accentuated with some make-up. Shadow the depression and highlight the edges.

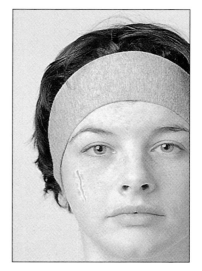

After continuous use, this method may damage the skin and leave a per-manent mark, so it is recommended only for very occasional use.

Scars can also be made with liquid latex adhesive:

1 Squeeze liquid latex adhesive on to a glass plate.

2 With a spatula or manicure tool, make required shape.

3 Allow this to dry, peel it off the plate and apply to the skin with spirit gum.

4 Accentuate scar with make-up, as for collodion scars.

With practice, very effective eye pouches or bags can also be made using this method.

One slight disadvantage of latex scars is that they are almost transparent. This can be corrected by adding a small amount of coloured pigment to the latex during the moulding stage. If you do not have powder pigments, scrape a small amount off the surface of a cake make-up with a scalpel. If the scar needs to be very livid, a scraping from the surface of a cake of dry rouge will work well.

Open cuts and wounds

Good latex wounds can usually be obtained from make-up suppliers but very often they are not exactly the type of wound that is required. Creating them yourself is usually more satisfactory.

1 First paint with spirit gum the area where the wound is to be placed.

2 Allow to dry.

3 Spread a thin layer of Derma Wax over the gummed area.

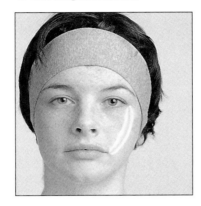

4 Using a spatula, carefully thin out the edge of the wax, making this as fine as possible.

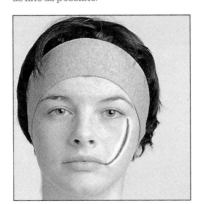

5 Make a cut in the wax, using the blunt edge of a modelling scalpel, and then very carefully open out the centre of the wound.

6 Colour the inside of the cut, using a dark-maroon lining colour on a brush. The lining colour may need to be softened with a little cold cream so that the colour can be gently brushed into the cut without disturbing the wax shape.

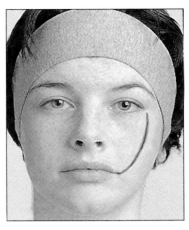

7 Paint a thin film of sealer over the wound and then allow it to dry completely.

8 Make-up the wound so that it blends well into the surrounding skin colour.

9 The cut can be accentuated with highlights that are applied along the edges.

10 Add stage blood into the cut, using an eye-dropper. Plastic blood, which dries very quickly, should be squeezed directly from its tube into the cut or wound.

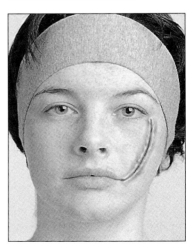

Special effects

Cuts

1 Paint the areas involved with spirit gum and let this dry.

2 Spread Derma wax over the wound area and flatten out the edges with a spatula.

3 Using the blunt edge of a modelling scalpel, make a cut and then open out the wound as required.

4 Paint the inside of the wound with a dark maroon lining colour. To make it more pliable and avoid damaging the latex, you may need to soften the lining colour with a little cold cream.

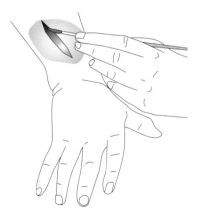

5 Paint over the completed wound with a thin film of sealer and leave this to thoroughly dry.

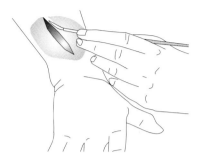

6 Disguise the edges of the wound with make-up to blend it into the surrounding skin.

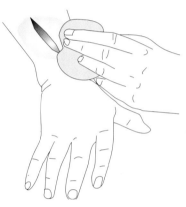

7 Highlight the edges of the cut to accentuate it.

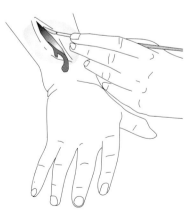

8 Stage blood can be applied with an eye-dropper or plastic blood squeezed out directly from the tube.

Bullet wounds

1 Paint a circle of spirit gum on to the skin and allow it to dry.

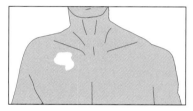

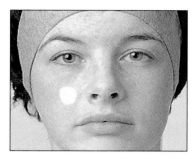

2 Spread a thin layer of Derma Wax over the gummed circle, thinning out the edges until they merge into the surrounding skin.

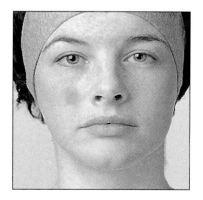

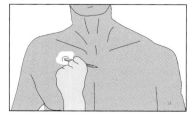

3 Press the blunt end of a pencil into the wax to make the required hole.

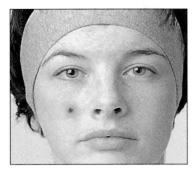

4 Paint inside the hole with a mixture of red and black lining colour to simulate blood and the charring of the flesh.

5 Cover the bullet wound with a thin film of sealer and add a thin trickle of blood, using a dark plastic blood.

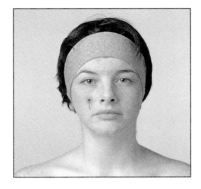

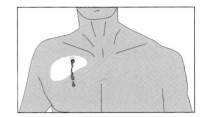

Blood flowing from the mouth

This is best achieved by using empty gelatine capsules purchased from your local pharmacy. Fill these with stage blood that is suitable for internal use. Check this with your make-up supplier. These capsules can be retained in the mouth and then simply crushed between the teeth to release a flow of blood.

External bleeding

A bloody nose or a sword cut can be simulated by using a small sponge, saturated in blood, which can be squeezed on to the area required. When it is not convenient for the actor to carry a blood sponge this might be concealed in the scenery or stage furniture until it is needed.

When blood is needed to seep out of, say, a shirt front, a blood sponge should be inserted into a small plastic bag with one or more small holes punched in one side. This package is

then taped to the actor's body, holes uppermost, underneath the clothing. All the actor then needs to do is to press on the area to release a slow ooze of blood through the holes. Remember to use blood that will not permanently stain the clothing! In any case, wash the costume as soon as possible.

The effect of flesh being cut and blood flowing from the cut can be simulated as follows:

1 Protect the sharp edge of the blade with cellophane tape.

2 Tape an eye-dropper filled with stage blood on to the underside of the blade, with the tip lying just alongside the cutting edge and the bulb conveniently placed by the hilt – so it can easily be depressed by the actor's thumb or first finger.

3 When the effect is required, the actor simply draws the protected blade edge along the flesh, keeping the eye dropper concealed on the underside. At the same time he or she depresses the bulb. A stream of blood will be drawn along the flesh from the tip of the eye dropper.

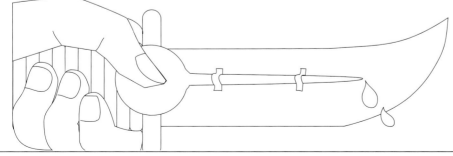

A non-retracting dagger using an eye dropper or pipette that contains artificial blood

Special effects

Making blood

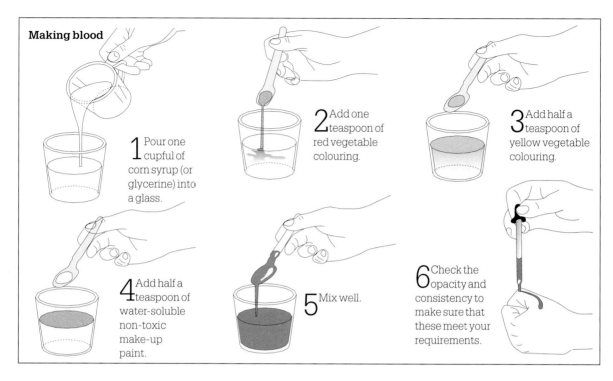

1 Pour one cupful of corn syrup (or glycerine) into a glass.

2 Add one teaspoon of red vegetable colouring.

3 Add half a teaspoon of yellow vegetable colouring.

4 Add half a teaspoon of water-soluble non-toxic make-up paint.

5 Mix well.

6 Check the opacity and consistency to make sure that these meet your requirements.

Burns

Burns can be simulated:

1 First stipple the area with maroon lining colour.

2 Cover this with a layer of liquid latex or sealer and allow it to dry completely.

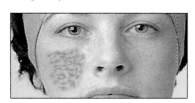

3 Break holes in the dry latex or sealer, lifting patches away from the skin to form broken blisters and peeling skin.

4 Black cake make-up, carefully stippled on, will help give the appearance of charring.

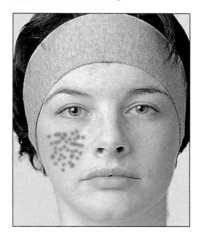

Black eyes and bruises

Fresh black eyes and bruises can be simulated with dark-red, purple, and blue-grey lining colours. Apply these colours in that order, one on top of the other, slightly decreasing the area covered with each application. This should be left unpowdered so the area looks very moist and inflamed.

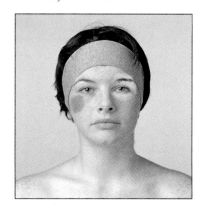

Special effects

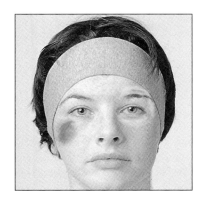

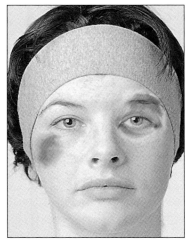

Older bruises and black eyes change colour as time passes; the inflammation fades and the surrounding areas of flesh become a rather yellowish-green. Start your application with a mixture of chrome-yellow and green, followed by blue-grey and purple. Finally add patches of dark red to the area closest to the eye or the centre of the bruise.

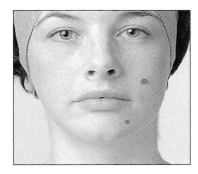

A swollen and colourful black eye can be simulated with make-up. Done correctly, this can look very effective and suitably three-dimensional

Warts and moles

Warts and moles can be created from many different materials, such as pre-formed latex pieces, Derma Wax, cotton balls and spirit gum (or even pieces of breakfast cereal, such as Rice Krispies or Puffed Wheat). These should be stuck to the skin with spirit gum and then suitably coloured.

When the wart needs to be hairy, you can attach the hairs to the material being used, before sticking it to the skin, but such detail is scarcely visible to the audience.

Gold teeth

A gold tooth, which looks very effective on a villain, pirate or bandit make-up, can easily be simulated by sticking a small piece of gold foil from a chocolate bar over the tooth, using spirit gum.

Perspiration

This is easily represented by spraying the face or body with glycerine, taking care to shield the eyes.

A greasy, sweaty appearance is achieved by rubbing the body with mineral oil.

A dirty, greasy look can be made by adding dark grease make-up to the oil as it is applied.

Long fingernails

Extra long fingernails, used for witches and Chinese mandarins, are difficult, if not impossible, to buy. You will need to cut them out of acetate or old photographic film. They can then be glued to the natural nails with false-fingernail glue or spirit gum, and coloured with nail varnish or the quick-drying acetate paint used by model makers.

Fingernails for witches can be bought or made from acetate or photographic film

Bronzed suntan effects

Although liquid body make-ups or body tints give a good colour to the skin, they tend to look dull and matt. The best tanned effect is achieved with those body-powder make-ups containing special ingredients which, if applied wet, allowed to dry, and then polished with the hands or a chiffon scarf, give off a gleaming shine.

Using masks

Tattoos

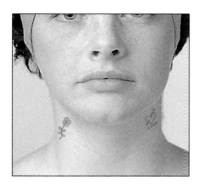

Tattoos can be drawn on to the skin with coloured eye-make-up pencils but remember that most tattoos are small works of art, so they need to be drawn very carefully. One method of getting a good shape for every performance is to trace the outline on to tracing paper and prick out the pattern with a thick needle. Then lay the pattern over the skin (which should first be lightly covered with a film of cold cream) and pat black face powder on to the paper. The face powder will go through the holes and so provide a dotted outline of the pattern, which you can then fill in with coloured pencils.

The tattoos illustrated on the opposite page make useful reference for tattoo design. You might like to experiment by tracing these and practising on a suitable 'victim'!

Henna-based temporary tattoos are now also widely available in a vast range of designs and can be very effective. How long they last depends upon the skin type and how frequent or vigorously the area is washed. They can survive for up to about three weeks so should 'see out' a week's run with no problem. See the *List of Suppliers* on page 152 for further details of these.

Using masks

Masks were one of the earliest forms of theatrical costume, hence the comic and tragic masks from Greek theatre that are still used as an icon to symbolise drama.

The face is the most dominant part of the human form, with facial expressions conveying the whole range of human emotions. This means that a mask can be a very powerful way to suggest a different creature or character and masks are still used in the dramatic, religious and festive ceremonies in many different cultures right around the world.

Masks are excellent when a dramatic effect is needed and marvellous for fast changes, transformations and for assuming non-human roles. They can eliminate a lot of time spent on conventional make-up as even a small mask can completely change the actor's appearance.

While not strictly within the realm of conventional make-up, if they are

Using masks

being used instead of this, or partially – to complement a make-up as a structure that reveals the face, or as an eye-mask only – then the make-up artist must be involved, if not in the mask's actual structure then at least in ensuring the masks co-ordinate with the rest of the make-ups and the style of the production. Close co-operation will be needed between the make-up artist, props and costumes, for any of these departments might create the mask.

Masks are static and can be uncomfortable to wear for long periods. Even the briefest eye mask restricts vision, feels hot under the lights and is distracting if it begins slip or to rub behind the ear lobes. Make sure that

---

Masks are good for . . .

1

Animals, birds, fish and insects. Fantasy creatures – vampires, robots, aliens, dragons, monsters, sprites, fairies, elves, demons and nursery rhyme characters.

2

Extreme human caricatures – such as pirates and gypsies, clowns, witches and witch doctors, ghosts and skulls – especially if there is insufficient time to alter make-up.

3

Non-human forms that have come to life: flowers and trees, Aladdin's lamp, sun, stars and moon.

4

Abstract ideas and emotions such as the elements (fire, earth, water), happiness and sorrow, fate and death.

---

the mask is as good a fit and as comfortable as possible.

If the actor has to be audible ensure that there is plenty of space for the sound to emerge. In general, half masks or open-faced head-dresses combined with appropriate make-up opinion are a better for a very busy actor with lots to say or sing.

Actors will also have to bear in mind that many masks are effective only when seen full face and this will effect the way they move.

Eye masks

A basic eye mask, the simplest of all masks, can be extended and added to in all sorts of ways to make a huge variety of masks. It can range then from the simple black eye covering for a robber to exotic bird faces with colourful beaks and crests of feathers – or a cat, or a butterfly.

Materials

Anything goes! Much depends on the style of the production, of course. Masks can be anything from a plain black eye mask to a tiger's face, an elegant creation for a masqued ball, a stocking pulled over the head or a bird's plumed extravaganza, made with flourishing glimmering feathers. Lightly boiled eggs can be scooped

out and the shells painted with PVA glue and paint to make prominent eyes or a rounded nose. Half ping-pong balls can also be used.

A cardboard mask

Many face and animal masks can be bought ready made but it is fun to experiment with making your own.

Human face masks are generally flat, curving when the elastic goes around the head. Animal masks, however, look more convincing if three-dimensional with a beak, snout or muzzle and ears that curl appropriately.

Papier mâché or cloth mâché

Papier mâché or cloth mâché (a cheesecloth and thinned glue mix is good for this purpose) can be built up on a clay form, onto a shape cut from a strong cardboard box, or over a balloon or a wire frame. A balloon based mask may be used as a solid head, or sliced in half and used to create two face masks.

Instead of papier mâché, a balloon can be surrounded with a criss-cross network of string that has been dipped in carpenter's glue.

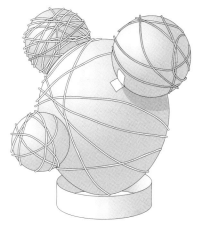

97

Using masks

Types of masks

Giant carnival masks

Masks can be flat or contoured

*Masks held on a stick
(These might be flat, contoured, full-face, half-face or eye masks–flat ones can also be reversible)*

Face masks

Half-face masks

Closely related to masks are head-dresses when part of the face is actually seen. These might be full head masks but with some or all of the face area cut away

Eye masks

There are also surround masks where the face is seen through a central cut-out – good for stars and flowers in children's shows

---

Consider using the following to make masks – and combining different materials

Fabric

Stockings

Paper and tissue

Card, cardboard and corrugated card

Lightweight wood

Cheesecloth

String

Straw

Metal foil

Large plastic containers

Fur fabric

Feathers

Papier mâché

Paper plates

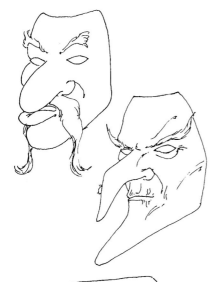

A simple mask shape can be adapted and built upon to create a huge range of character faces. These can be worn comfortably because of the snug fit created by using an individually cast mask

Full head masks

Making a mould

Masks can also be constructed on top of a mould made of clay, or plaster and sandcast, or created directly over the actor's face so that the fit is excellent. Dental mould applied over the actor's face sets into a rubbery material and reproduces minute details. The mould can be painted and used as a solid life mask but is generally used as a mould around which other masks can be formed, the interior surface of which will then fit the actor perfectly. The new masks can be modelled with all sorts of new features like huge noses or bulging eyes. Moulds like this can also be made with FlexWax.

For a quicker method, the actor's face can be covered with petroleum jelly, with tissue covering any facial hair. Two or three layers of small wet plaster bandage squares are smoothed directly on to the actor's face to fit all the contours closely. This mould will set in about ten minutes and can then be used to create a positive cast in plaster of Paris.

The features and other details on a mask can be painted directly on to the mask or made from all sorts of household items or craft materials, which can include Plasticine or Fimo (polymer clay), card, felt, clay, buttons, bottle tops, egg boxes, sequins and wire.

If required, hair can be made from a vast range of materials such as shredded fabric, fur fabric, wool, raffia, twine or rope, curtain 'tie-back' cord, paper, feathers, wood shavings, wire, springs and glitter foil.

Masks can be made to sit on top of an actor's head to allow him or her to see and speak clearly if the role demands this. This type of mask needs to be relatively light and well balanced. Foam rubber is useful because it is not too top heavy. The face make-up will need to co-ordinate well with the mask style and colours.

International characters

In an ideal world, actors of appropriate nationalities and skin types will be available to perform characters from different races – so no drastic make-up changes will be needed. This is certainly the case nowadays in the professional theatre.

However, the world is rarely ideal and, especially in small-scale amateur productions, there may be circumstances when the make-up artist is called upon to make up actors so that they can perform roles that require another skin type.

There are also certain parts, like Shakespeare's Othello, that present such an exciting challenge to actors from many nations that they are regularly played by performers of a different skin type to the role.

In the same way, productions such as Gilbert and Sullivan's *Mikado* will generally require the entire cast to be given stylized make-up – in this case, Japanese.

So, for those cases when it is considered appropriate to use make-up to change nationality, here follows an analysis of significant differences in skin types and facial features which can help denote race and nationality and some suggestions on how to create make-ups to suggest these differences.

The purpose of any stage make-up is not necessarily to be an absolutely accurate 'copycat' from life but to create the right impression, to convey the 'feeling' of a role. This applies to ethnic or national make-up as much as any other kind. There are certain characteristics of every skin type and national trends that can be suggested – or exaggerated – in order to convey the right impression to the audience.

Analyse the types of face

Unlike film make-up, stage make-up is not seen in close-up so it is the overall feeling that must be analysed and understood before the make-up is created in detail. As with any other make-up, the degree of exaggeration that is required will depend upon stage size, the strength of the lighting, and the proximity of the character to the audience.

Obviously there are many books on stage make-up and it is useful to study these in order to understand the necessary techniques, but it is also useful to build up your own 'dossier' of information on national characteristics. Collect photographs of people of different races and skin types from magazines so that you can create a useful portfolio for future reference. Group similar races and types of face together and analyse the differences between these various groups.

Check out the following:

Skin colour

Hair colour

Shape of face

Eye colour

Eye shape

Shape and size of other features

Special characteristics

Decide how important or dominant these differences are. For example, would coloured contact lenses to change the eye colour be useful? Would such a fine detail be detected by the audience?

As ever, much depends on the intimacy of the theatre and what detail the audience can actually see. However, it is also important that the actors are comfortable with the approach to the make-up and that its effectiveness will give them increased confidence in their role portrayal.

Decide:

1

What are the vital elements of this character/role that must be conveyed?

2

What racial characteristics are most important?

3

What detail can the audience really see?

4

What will help the actor to feel right and so boost his or her portrayal?

There follow some specific make-up treatments. Obviously there is insufficient space within the scope of this book to cover every race – and every age-group therein – so just a few of the more likely portrayals are examined. This is where your own portfolio of faces will be useful to augment the more regular make-ups with information on those less likely to occur so frequently.

In all cases, try on wigs before making up – to check fit and position. Then remove and replace only when facial make-up is completed.

Oriental make-up

Madam Butterfly

The Mikado

Chu Chin Chow

Emperor and the Nightingale

The Firebird

Aladdin (the Genie)

Also certain productions or scenes set in the Second World War, such as *Bridge over the River Kwai* and *The Long, the Short and the Tall*

Oriental complexions actually vary greatly and can range from very pale olive to dark yellowish-brown. Pure yellow foundations should never be used, except for very stylised make-ups, such as those that might be implemented for certain characters in *The Mikado*.

The other mistaken idea is that oriental eyes slope obliquely upwards. This is an optical illusion. Oriental eyes are in fact almond-shaped, horizontal and narrow, with a tendency, if anything, to slope downwards. Again, it can be very useful to examine closely the collection of images in your portfolio rather than making assumptions or generalisations.

Generally speaking, the Japanese skin is slightly darker and more olive than the paler Chinese skin, The Japanese eye is widest at the inner corner, giving it a decided downward slope. The Japanese jawline is usually strong with a long upper lip.

In both races the features are very smooth. The easiest way to achieve

this is with an even and slightly heavy application of cake make-up, which will give an overall flatness to the face.

The most noticeable and striking thing about the oriental eye is the shallowness and flatness of the orbital socket. This flatness can be simulated by applying a strong highlight to the entire orbital area or by using artificial oriental eyelids. If the character is young, the hair (or wig) should be very straight, black and shiny.

Oriental eyelids

Artificial eyelids tend to close the eye so much that all expression can be lost. This is particularly problematic if the performance is taking place in a very large theatre.

On the other hand, it can be difficult to create the appearance of an oriental eye with just highlight and shadow, especially if an actor's eye socket is very deep.

Made-to-measure false eyelids are very effective but are expensive and difficult to obtain.

Often the best solution is to create your own oriental eyelids from adhesive tape or fine chamois leather.

You will need a piece of surgical adhesive tape or chamois leather about 50 x 28mm (2.5 x 1.125 inches).

1 Cut out the shape shown by heavy line A.

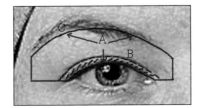

2 If using adhesive tape, powder shaded area B on the false lid.

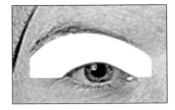

3 Press or stick the lid into place, covering the end of each eyebrow.

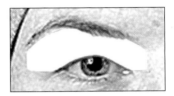

4 Using the end of a tail comb, release eyebrow hairs at C.

5 Emphasis the puffy look of oriental eyelids with highlights.

6 The false lid should now be made up with base colour.

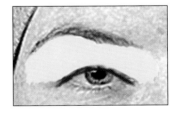

7 Now shade along the edge of the eye opening and highlight the centre of the lid to create the slightly swollen look of an oriental eyelid.

Young oriental woman

Young oriental woman

Madam Butterfly

The Mikado
(The Three Little Maids)

This make-up might be used for *Madam Butterfly* or certain characters in *The Mikado*. It would not be suitable for geisha girls, however, who need totally artificial make-up with white faces. The step-by-step routine that follows shows how to apply a more natural oriental make-up, using just light and shade.

1 Block out the end of the eyebrows and apply a smooth even layer of cake make-up over entire face and throat with a cosmetic sponge.

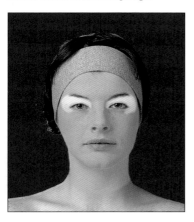

2 Highlight entire orbital area with white cake make-up, using a 6mm (0.25 inch) flat-ended sable brush. Carry highlight up over the blocked-out eyebrow and down over the edge of the eye socket below the outer end of the eye.

3 Highlight and shade nose to flatten and shorten it.

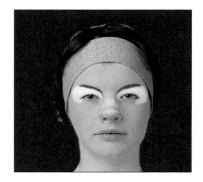

4 Now sketch in the eyebrows. Start at a point low down near the nose, below the natural growth of the eyebrow hair. Then curve the line up in a crescent shape, stopping short of the end of the browbone.

5 Draw a fine, black line along the edge of the top lid, very close to the roots of the lashes. At the outer corner of the eye, extend the line in a slightly downward direction before winging it up under the strong highlight on the browbone. Fade out the top edge of the line.

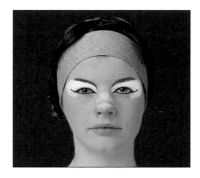

6 At the inner corner of the eye, drop the line of black under the edge of the top lid, continuing it down over the inner corner of the eye to simulate the oriental fold.

7 Darken the inside edge of the lower lid with kohl pencil to narrow eye shape.

8 Add a small triangle of black lining at outer corner of eye to blend with upper line.

9 Accentuate highlight immediately above fold with an extra touch of white cake make-up.

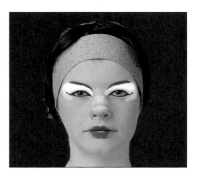

10 Paint in the mouth with an exaggerated rosebud shape. Highlight centre of lower lip for extra fullness. Deepen shadow under lower lip with a brown eyebrow pencil.

11 Brush on cake rouge at an oblique angle over the cheekbones to accentuate the flatness of the bone structure.

12 Put on the wig and carefully fasten this into place.

13 Make up hands and exposed skin with a toning body make-up. You might add false fingernails to lengthen and slim the hand.

Colour guide

Foundation
Mix ivory with peach or yellow groups for Chinese, and ivory with peach, olive or yellow for Japanese skin types

Highlights
White or ivory group

Shading
Olive-brown or lake groups

Lips and cheeks
Light or medium-red groups

Young oriental man

Apart from the operas previously mentioned, young male Japanese characters appear in several plays set in the Second World War and musicals such as *Chu Chin Chow.*

1 Apply artificial oriental eyelids (see page 101). Use the false lid to block out the ends of the eyebrows.

2 Smooth an even layer of foundation over the entire face and throat. Cake make-up can be used for a stylised look but cream-stick or grease will look more natural and blend easily over the false lids.

3 Now highlight the false lids. Emphasize both the centre and the overhang.

4 Apply a shadow along the edge of the artificial lid. Extend the shadow downward at the outer end of the false piece.

5 Apply a narrow highlight along the edge of the lower lid, immediately below the lashes. Add a shadow below this highlight.

6 Highlight and shade the nose to flatten and shorten it as much as possible. Try to keep the shadows at the sides of the nostrils as horizontal as possible.

7 Highlight top lip to make it as long as possible. A thin strip of moistened cosmetic sponge can be inserted under the upper lip at the top of the gum to accentuate this illusion.

8 Paint on a shorter, fuller lip shape. Keep upper lip narrow and dark and the lower lip full and rounded. Deepen the shadow below the lower lip with brown eyebrow pencil.

9 Brush on dark, shading rouge at an oblique angle over the back of the cheekbone to help flatten the bone structure.

10 Put on the wig and secure this.

The ageing oriental

11 Make up the hands as well as all exposed skin areas with body make-up to tone with the face.

Colour guide

Foundation
Mix ivory or olive groups with warm tan or yellow groups

Highlights
White or ivory groups

Shading
Olive-brown mixed with lake groups

Lips and cheeks
Lake groups

The ageing oriental

The ageing oriental has a pale yellow-white skin with soft, thinning grey hair that practically blends into the skin colour.

1 Both male and female make-ups will need false oriental eyelids. Apply these first.

2 Drain all the natural colour from the skin by using a very pale ivory foundation.

For men . . .

3 Apply shadows and highlights to give an exaggerated skull-like appearance to the face. Set with translucent face powder.

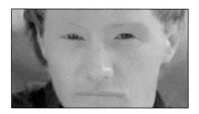

4 Add a very small colourless mouth with deep wrinkles.

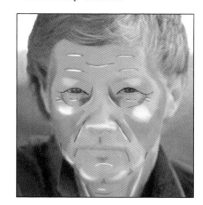

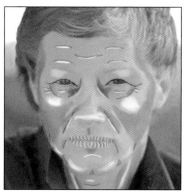

5 Use a bald wig with long, wispy side hair. Hide blender edge with shading at temples and exaggerated forehead lines.

6 Add a thin wispy beard and moustache. Use thin sections of straightened real crepe hair rather than wool crepe.

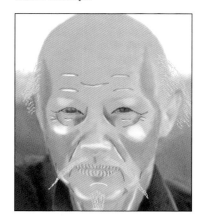

7 Make up the hands. Give a skeletal look to the fingers and then add long fingernails.

For women . . .

3 Add highlights and shadows to suggest heavy folds and puffiness. The cheek pads should look full and the neck folds heavy.

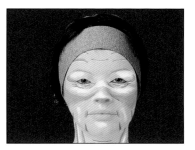

4 Now apply a small dark mouth. Exaggerate the puffiness at the mouth corners.

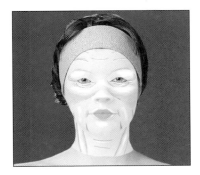

5 Stipple some broken veins under the cheek pads.

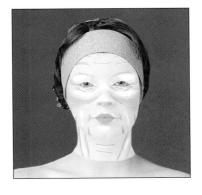

6 Use a wig with very fine hair over a balding pate; or use one dressed back into a tight bun with a blender front to add height to the forehead.

7 Make up the hands with very pale, ivory body make-up.

Asiatic make-up

Adaptations of *Kim* and
The Jungle Book

The King and I

Notes on special features

Change the skin and hair colour – and the shape of eyebrows and eyes. These are the most easily recognised Asian features.

Asiatic eyebrows are generally well defined, heavy, and straight above deep-set, almond-shaped eyes.

The skin around the eye should be darker than the rest of the face. This imbues an intense, mystical look to the eyes of Asiatic Indians, an effect which is heightened by the use of kajal in the eye itself.

For Asiatic Indians, the skin near the mouth should be dark and the beard-line should be dark and strong. The skin at the edge of the hairline should be given the same darkening as the eye and mouth areas.

Caste marks
All Hindu women except widows are likely to wear caste marks. Often they are just small red dots but they may be ornate and bejewelled. Apply a caste mark to centre of the forehead, between the ends of the brows. The blunt end of a grease liner gives the ideal shape. Alternatively, the blunt end of a pencil or the head of a large nail rubbed with colour both make excellent substitutes. Men may also use caste marks.

Married Bengali women redden the centre parting of their hair.

Asiatic Indian hair is very dark, but is not like the intense blue-black of the oriental people.

The Hindu male may shave his hair close to the scalp, leaving a single lock at the crown.

The Sikh male never cuts his hair, concealing it beneath his turban. The beard is left uncut and the more sophisticated Sikh curls it around elastic in a tight roll close to the jaw.

Asiatic Indian man

Indian Ink
by Tom Stoppard

If a turban is being worn, a wig may not be necessary but any exposed hair must be darkened with spray.

1 Try on the turban or wig.

2 Apply a very dark olive-brown foundation in a fine film over the entire face.

Asiatic Indian man

3 With the same colour, darken the areas around the eyes, nose, mouth and hairline.

4 Using a pale yellow-toned highlighter, emphasise bone structure. Apply long highlight down the nose and highlight the top lid; slightly extend this line at the outer end.

5 Powder all over, especially if using grease make-up.

6 Sketch in the eyebrows with black pencil; start high above the nose with the inner ends fairly close together. Keep the shape as straight and as horizontal as possible, emphasising the growth of hair under the browbone area.

7 Strongly outline top and bottom lids, starting at the inner corner of the eye. Carry the colour around the eye to meet at the outer corner. Extend line straight out to give a horizontal look.

8 Apply black mascara.

9 Clearly define mouth. Add black or dark-blue to intensify the colour. Outline lips with pencil.

10 With a coarse stippling sponge, stipple the beard and moustache area with black to emphasise the beardline.

11 Replace wig or turban and secure firmly in place. In some cases it may be possible to colour and re-style the natural hair, in which case it should be sprayed with brilliantine dressing to impart a gloss.

12 Make up hands and any exposed body areas.

Sikh men

This Asian make-up can be adapted for a Sikh man. Add a luxuriant beard and moustache and perhaps an aquiline nose shape with nose putty.

Asiatic women

The King and I
(the king's wives)

1 Apply a thin film of olive-brown grease or cream-stick make-up over the entire face.

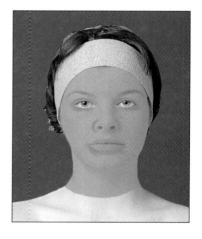

2 Darken the areas around eye sockets, the nostrils, the sides of the mouth and along the hairline by adding extra foundation.

3 Thoroughly powder with translucent face powder.

4 Apply a film of a clear, golden-tan cake make-up over the face, using a sponge.

5 Using a lighter tone of cake make-up, apply highlights to nose, chin and cheekbones.

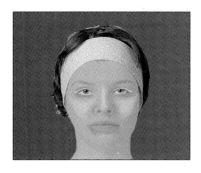

6 Apply the same highlight colour to top eyelid. Extend this out horizontally beyond outer corner of eye.

7 Outline eye with black eyeliner, opening lines at the outer end in a parallel shape.

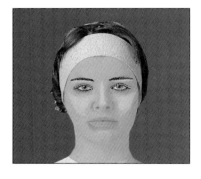

8 Starting at inner corner of eye, draw a contour crease line around the back of top eyelid. Extend this at outer end, parallel with top eyeliner. Blend away top edge upwards over browbone.

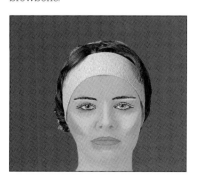

9 Sketch eyebrows in a clear outline. Follow the same horizontal pattern as eyelining and contour creases.

10 Apply a highlight along browbone between the eyebrow and contour crease. Extend it horizontally at outer end. Add a touch of highlight along top of eyebrow.

11 Make up both the top and bottom lashes with several coats of black mascara.

12 Add kohl pencil to the inside edge of the lower lid. Extra intensity can be added to the eye make-up by applying kohl pencil to the inner edge of the top lid too, underneath the lashes. Gently roll up the top eyelid and lift back with the fingertips; then apply kohl pencil.

13 Outline lips with brown eyebrow pencil. Fill in lip colour with a number 6 filbert brush.

14 Shade the cheekbones with blusher. An Indian Asiatic Hindu woman might need a caste mark (see page 105).

15 Replace wig. Make up hands and all exposed areas of skin.

Black make-up

Othello

A Streetcar named Desire

The Crucible

When a Caucasian performer is called upon to play a black role, such as in *Othello*, it is necessary to adapt certain characteristics. Study the actor's face carefully to discover which features can most easily be changed.

Do not make the skin too dark since this will prevent you from broadening and flattening the features with shading. If a very dark base colour is highlighted, the highlight tends to look chalky and dead and to sit on the surface – just as light colours do when applied to a naturally dark skin. If you study an black complexion, you will see that the natural highlights have a pale, almost translucent appearance.

Wear protective plastic gloves when applying make-up, to avoid staining fingertips and nails.

General guidelines

1 First apply cake make-up with a cosmetic sponge moistened with a transparent, liquid body make-up instead of water. This transparent liquid make-up can be removed from the skin only with soap and water, so the dark make-up cannot be accidentally rubbed off to reveal pale flesh beneath.

2 To create highlights, the cake make-up can be rubbed away with a cotton pad moistened with the body tint. This removes the cake make-up but leaves behind the lighter, transparent body tint.

Black make-up

3 If a stronger, lighter highlight is required, use a pad of cotton moistened with water, which will also remove some of the tint.

4 Shadows can be applied by painting them on with black cake make-up. Use a sable brush that has been moistened with the transparent body make-up.

5 The body can also be made up with this combination of cake make-up and transparent body make-up. When it is dry, the surface can be polished to a high sheen, ideally with a piece of silk chiffon.

6 The eyes should look large and white in contrast to the dark skin. A natural effect can be achieved by lining the inside edge of the lid with brown kohl pencil.

7 Black hair is usually short and close to the head so unless this is a wild Afro look, dress the actor's hair as flat as possible or use a wig.

Young black man

As in *Othello*

1 Try on the wig. Keep the hairline low on the forehead and ensure that all natural hair is concealed.

2 Remove the wig and apply cake make-up with transparent body make-up.

3 On the nose, chin, browbone, cheekbones and jawline, highlight base colour by rubbing away the cake make-up with body tint or water on a small cotton ball.

4 Apply black pancake on a 6mm (0.25 inch) sable brush, moistened with body tint which will shade the face strongly.

5 Draw on strong eyebrows with black pencil, rubbing through the drawn-on shape with a fingertip to give a blurred outline.

6 Heavily outline the eyes with black pencil or lining colour. Blend away the edges.

7 Apply kohl pencil on to inside edge of lower lid.

8 Make up top lashes with black mascara or masque.

9 Outline lips with black eyebrow pencil, enlarging shape. Darken lips with pencil, making top lip quite dark. Cover mouth with cake make-up. Using a 3mm (0.125 inch) sable brush, draw a line of white lining colour around enlarged lip shape. Intensify shadow under lower lip with a black pencil.

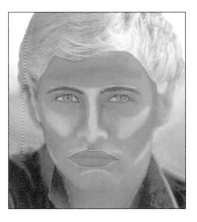

10 Replace wig and fasten with spirit gum.

Black make-up

11 Broaden nostrils with nose plugs. These can be made from the tips from two pacifiers or baby bottle nipples. Blacken the insides with eyebrow pencil and, once in place, conceal edges with black eyebrow pencil.

12 Make up hands and all exposed body areas with cake and body-tint. Remove cake colour from the palms of the hands and soles of the feet with a cotton ball moistened with tint or water.

13 Keep any facial hair sparse and close to the skin.

Colour guide

Foundation
Dark-brown groups
applied with dark body
tint

Lips
Lake groups if warmer
colour is needed

Eyes
Black eyebrow pencil
and kohl

Black woman

Tituba in *The Crucible*

---

1 Try on wig. Make sure hair is fairly low, to help shorten the forehead.

2 Apply cake make-up with transparent body tint. Take colour around the back of the neck, behind ears and well beyond wig line.

3 Colour inside the ears, using a sable brush.

4 Cover lips with foundation.

5 Using a cotton ball moistened with transparent body tint, rub away cake make-up from areas to be highlighted.

6 Apply shading with black cake and tint.

7 Widen nose by drawing in the nostril line about 3mm (0.125 inch) away from the natural crease. Keep the shadows on the sides of the nose well apart.

8 Shade chin so as to give it maximum width.

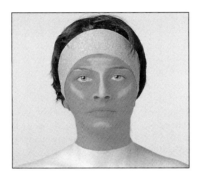

9 Darken skin around the eye.

10 Make high shadows in the cheek hollows. Keep them well to the back of the face to add width and heighten the cheekbones.

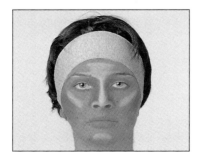

11 Sketch in strong brows.

12 Shade in contour creases at the back of the top lids; fade colour up over browbone.

13 Outline eyes strongly with black pencil or eyeliner, blending away edges.

14 Apply black mascara to top and bottom lashes and add false lashes, if required. Then apply kohl pencil to the inside edge of the lower lids.

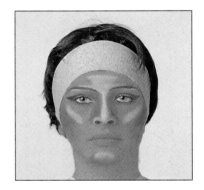

15 Using black pencil, blacken inside nostrils. Continue out over the edge of the openings so they seem larger.

16 With black pencil, draw an outline around lips to enlarge their shape; work a little pencil over top lip.

17 Apply lip colour over this new shape. Add a touch of highlight to the centre of the lower lip to increase fullness.

18 With an 3mm (0.125 inch) sable brush, draw white liner above outline of top lip. Carefully blend it upwards away from lips. Intensify shadow under bottom lip, using black eyebrow pencil.

Arabian make-up

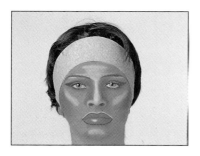

19 Replace the wig and fasten this into place.

20 Make up hands and any other exposed areas. Use the same combination of cake and body tint as on the face. Cotton moistened with tint will rub away the cake from the palms of the hands so that they are a pinky brown.

Portraying older black roles

The best base for this type of make-up is either a cream-stick or greasepaint.

A warm dark base is very difficult to age. The best colours are very dark olive-browns, with yellow undertones rather than red.

The make-up application is very similar to ageing a white character – except that each shadow and highlight must broaden and flatten the face, as well as suggesting age.

Sir Laurence Olivier as Othello

Colour guide

Foundation
For light colouring use warm-tan groups or olive-brown groups, applied with medium-dark body tint.
For very dark colouring, use dark-brown groups applied with dark body tint.

Cheeks
Dark-red or lake groups

Lips
Dark-red or lake groups or lipstick of choice.

Arabian make-up

Terence Rattigan's play *Ross* needs both Arab and Turkish characters but the make-up discussed here is geared to romantic characters as in musicals like *Kismet*.

Arabian characters are frequently found in the theatre, particularly in musicals and fairy tales. The make-up on page 111 is deliberately flamboy-

ant. It would need a little toning down for a straight role.

The stereotyped stage image of the Arab sheikh is hawk-nosed, lean-faced and usually bearded and moustached, but there are, of course, many other types of Arab face. The make-up described here can easily be adapted by changing the shape of the beard, the nose, or the eyebrow – to suit the particular part being played.

Most of the Arabian characters in light entertainment wear national costume and their hair is covered by a turban or head-dress – so wigs are not always necessary. By contrast, in straight plays, the Arab is often portrayed as a westernised character. In these cases the hair should be dark and wavy, and heavily brilliantined. Check your 'faces portfolio' for suitable reference.

Arabian sheikh or sultan

Arabian Nights

Aladdin

Dick Whittington
(the ruler that Dick's cat helps by killing the rats)

The Champion of Paribanou

1 Apply a false nose, using either nose putty or a latex piece.

Arabian make-up

2 Use shading to slim face. Strongly accentuate bone structure.

3 Highlight shadows sharply. Clearly emphasise cheekbones and browbones.

4

5 Sketch in eyebrows with a black pencil. The shape should add to hawk-like appearance.

6 Outline eyes with black liner or eye pencil. Use a downward extension of the lines in inner corner and a strong, upward winging shape at outer corner.

7 Draw in a contour crease with liner or pencil. Blend away top edge in an outward winging pattern. Mascara fair lashes.

8 Strongly define mouth with dark-lake liner. Deepen lips with black or dark-blue.

9 Apply beard and moustache, and wig, if required.

10 Finally, add an Arabian head-dress to complete the sheik transformation.

Egyptian Pharaoh

This make-up can be adapted for an Egyptian Pharaoh.

Apply exaggerated eye make-up and outlines.

Leave the chin clean-shaven but then add an obviously false beard.

Arabian harem girl

To accompany the very theatrical sheikh – the glamorous slave or harem girl is a regular character in revues, dance and ballet, and pantomimes.

She is, undeniably, a theatrical invention. This character has a totally artificial face, and the actress or make-up artist need have no inhibitions about what may be used to achieve the end result. Glitter, jewels, outrageously false lashes, gold and silver make-up can all be added – so long as the result is beautiful, glamorous, and very seductive.

Slaves were captured from every part of the world known to their captors, so they can be of any colour or race, and

111

Arabian make-up

the more exotic and mysterious they look, the better. The slaves can be fair like the Persian women who bleached their skins and stayed out of the sun; they can be beautifully tanned; or dark and bronzed like the Amazons; or oriental; or black.

If the women who play this type of part are dancers, then the make-up can be very balletic, giving scope for elaborate, exotic eye make-up. A winged-up, fly-away shape looks dramatic and 'eastern' but it must be done clearly and cleanly.

Notes on an exotic make-up

1 Before starting the make-up, the end of the natural brows must either be plucked or blocked out to allow eye make-up to be swept up and out towards the temples.

2 You can use any colours you choose for the eyes, so long as they are strong and clean.

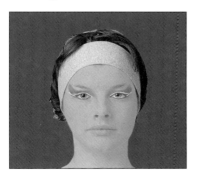

3 Iridescent and metallic eye shadows and face glitter will be particularly good, especially if the costume is very glittery or shiny.

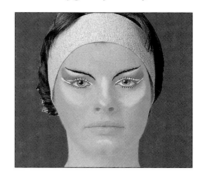

4 A strong angle of shading and highlighting on the cheekbones works well, with the eyelines, eyebrows and eyeshadow all following the same angle – upward and outward toward the temples.

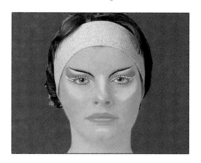

5 Lips should be full and sensuously curved. Use strong light colours with plenty of lip gloss.

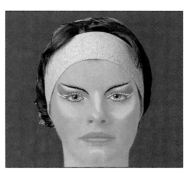

Slave-girl costumes are often flimsy and revealing, so good body make-up is essential. If the show is to have a long run, it may be worth while using a sun-bed or artificial tanning lotion to achieve a good tan and so obviate the need for nightly body make-up. If make-up has to be used, cake or liquid body-make-up is better than transparent tints. These give the skin a smooth, glamorous finish. Gleaming body powder can also look very effective as can the addition of body gels (or face make-up) containing glitter.

Jewels can be applied to the face. Use spirit gum or liquid latex adhesive. The best type of jewels are those that have a flat back so that they will adhere easily to the skin. Apply spirit gum to both the jewel and the skin and allow it to become tacky before pressing the jewel into place. Spirit gum, however, must be removed with care after the show. Dissolve it with solvent and then gently massage away with a facial tissue. Be very careful not to get the solvent into the eye – the best way to do this is for the actress to lean well forward, putting the head down so that the browbone is below the eye. Then carefully use the solvent.

Jewellery will help the glamorous effect

Mediterranean make-up

Mediterranean make-up

Dona Rosita the Spinster

Shirley Valentine

Saturday, Sunday,
Monday

The Talented Mr Ripley

The Noble Spaniard

Don Juan

Yerma

Carmen

Royal Hunt of the Sun

The Mediterranean or Latin races include Spaniards, Portuguese, Italians, Greeks and South American characters of European descent. These nationalities have many characteristics in common, so the make-up can be easily adapted to suit the country of origin. Try to create a strong bone structure and dark golden-olive complexions. The hair should look very dark and glossy and the lips strong and sensual.

Mediterranean woman

Carmen

Also gypsy characters

Many Spanish, Italian and South-American roles, like Carmen, are depicted as strong and fiery. This should be reflected in the make-up.

1 First apply a dark, golden-tan foundation. Then add some strong highlighting and shading to emphasise the bone structure.

2 Powder with iridescent translucent face powder.

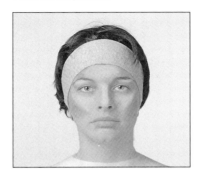

3 Sketch in eyebrows, lifting them as high as possible. Make them dark and well defined.

4 Apply a strong eyeshadow to the top eyelid and along the edge of the lower lid (beneath the lashes) to enlarge the eye as much as possible.

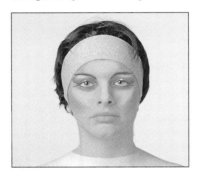

5 Highlight the centre of top lid to give it prominence.

6 Outline eyes with dark eyeliner. Keep outer ends wide apart in a fishtail shape.

7 Use white eyeliner along the inside edge of the lower lid. Continue it out between the open ends of eyeliner at outer corner of eye.

8 Mascara top and bottom lashes. Apply false lashes if required.

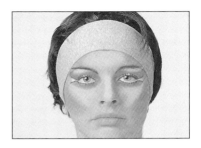

9 Outline mouth with a dark-red lip pencil or lip colour. Fill in the centre of the lips with clear bright red. Apply lip gloss.

10 Accentuate the cheek shading with dark shading rouge. Add plenty of accent rouge to the cheekbones to give a good strong lift to the make-up.

11 Dress hair in the required style or use a wig.

Mediterranean make-up

A hairstyle (or wig) with glossy dark hair and elaborate curls around the face will be appropriate for a South-American or a Spanish character.

Dressing the hair flatter to the head and taking it back into a chignon will immediately make this character appear far less flamboyant. If a neutral brown eyeshadow is then used and the lipstick and the rouge are more subdued, then the make-up can suggest an austere Greek woman or an Italian peasant.

Mediterranean man

The Noble Spaniard

Royal Hunt of the Sun
(Pizzaro and his soldiers)

1 Nose putty or a false nose can be used to strengthen the profile, particularly for an aristocratic character.

2 Next apply a dark, golden-tan foundation.

3 Add corrective highlighting and strong shading to exaggerate the bone structure. Latin characters tend to be portrayed as having strong, fiery temperaments and this must be reflected in the make-up. The bone structure should be emphasised as much as possible.

4 Powder with iridescent translucent face powder.

5 Sketch in very dark, wide brows. Keep the pattern of growth low under the browbone. Maintain the same width along the whole of the brow. Slightly decrease density of growth at the outer end. A few strokes of pencil added between the brows will give a heavy, menacing look, if this is what is required.

6 The eyes need to be very dark and fascinating so rather more eye make-up can be used than is usual for a man. Give top lid a strong highlight and then sink in the contour crease with a strong line of black pencil or lining colour, fading it up toward browbone.

7 Line both the top and the bottom lids strongly with black; open the outer corners into a fishtail shape. Blend away the edges of these lines to give a dark, smouldering look. Men with fair lashes should darken them with black mascara.

8 For large stages and operatic roles, white lining can be added along inside edge of lower lid and between open ends of eyeliner.

9 Lips need to be made very strong and quite full. Where the outline is weak, the mouth should be lined with dark-brown pencil, fading colour inward toward middle of mouth. Fill in centre with a dark brown-red.

10 Hair is a very important element of the overall effect. Wigs for this type of make-up can look very artificial. It may be better to darken the natural hair with a water rinse and then re-style. Use plenty of brilliantine dressing to give the hair a high gloss.

11 Add long sideburns that run down the sides of the face and curve forward under cheekbones. Accompanied by a thin, dark moustache, this look will be immediately recognisable as being typically South

American Indians

American or Spanish. Real hairpieces are the best to use, especially for small stages and for theatre in the round. In larger theatres, however, moustaches and sideburns can be quite convincingly drawn in with black eyebrow pencil. Sketch them in with small hairlike strokes applied one on top of another; gradually build up the shape and density.

12 Most Latin men have strong, well-marked beardlines. This gives a dark, swarthy appearance but, when using make-up to simulate this, great care should be taken not to make the character look unsuitably villainous. (See also page 82 on how to apply stubble.)

Greek man

Shirley Valentine
(the taverna owner)

Greek men have very similar colouring to the other Latin races. However, they can look quite different because of their hair which is is often curly and full. Their moustaches, too, are usually large and luxuriously flamboyant.

This is one of those make-ups that can be all too easily stereotyped. Much depends on the style of the production and particular roles but generally it is better to underplay the effects, especially as the costumes will convey the character's nationality quite clearly.

American Indians

Calamity Jane

Hiawatha

Annie Get Your Gun

1 Apply foundation. Choose one with tan-red tones but ensure that it is not too orange or artificial. Experiment first to find what works best and most suits the particular actor's complexion.

2 Add strong highlighting and shading to emphasise bone structure really well, giving particular attention to the cheekbones.

3 If ritualistic or war paint is required, use russet and deep blue or purple tones Be careful not to overdo the effect or to detract from the face's strong bone structure. Add highlights to these patterns.

4 Powder with iridescent translucent face powder.

5 Sketch in strong eyebrows. Make these bushier for an older male.

6 Also for older characters, add pencil strokes and highlighting to emphasise the vertical furrows between the brows.

7 Line both top and bottom eyelids with black. Sweep the top line down a little before blending away the edges of these lines. For older characters, a stronger Oriental fold might be suggested.

8 Line the mouth with dark-brown pencil, and then gently fade this colour inwards.

9 For female characters fill in lip shape with a russet lipstick.

10 The hair – or wig – needs to be blue-black and very glossy for young roles. A white wig can work well for an old character. Hair might be worn loose under a hairband or dressed in plaits.

11 Make sure any exposed body areas are made up suitably so as to tone in with the face make-up.

Before creating make-ups, it is useful to collect photographs and illustrations, such as these two examples of American Indian images.

Special shows and styles

Many professional modern productions employ an artistic director who oversees all the visual elements of the show – such as the scenery, costumes and make-up – to ensure that there is close co-ordination between all these aspects of production and that the style or theme of the play is followed through consistently.

Whether or not this is the case in your group (it may be the director instead who suggests overall artistic guidelines), there are general decisions that must be taken before planning any of the visual aspects of the production – including the make-up.

> For example:
>
> What size is the stage?
>
> How strong is the lighting?
>
> What is the overall style of the production?
>
> Does the make-up need to be natural, exaggerated or fantastic?

The various types of play discussed in this section show how the approach to the make-up will vary. While it presents only a selection of just a few types of production – and specific make-ups from a vast range of possible characters – the basis for decision making will be explored and can be applied to the entire range of possible play types and characters.

While there is space here to look at just a few make-ups in detail, the principals of fantasy versus realism – and how each can be achieved – will remain consistent in every theatrical presentation.

Small stage

A small stage will generally mean that the character is close to the audience. Make-up will need to be as natural as possible, taking into account the style of play, the reality of the characters and the strength of the lighting. Even on a very small intimate stage, however, if the lighting is powerful, the make-up will need to gain strength to compensate for this or the cast will all look anaemic. So there are no hard and fast rules.

Each venue will make its own demands – as does each play. If the production is being played in the round, for example, or involves a good deal of audience participation, then, this close proximity to the audience will become a factor. In a straight play where there is close contact with the audience, realism may require a lesser degree of make-up – but if the show is stylised or 'over the top' then strong make-up, or even shock tactics, may be in order!

Large stage

A large stage will generally mean that the character is somewhat removed from the audience. Make-up will need to be stronger and detailing will be less important.

In an ideal world, you will have an opportunity to test out the make-up in the venue beforehand with full lighting; then it can be adapted to suit.

However, it is a much more likely scenario that you will be unable to bring all the necessary elements together (venue, lighting, actors and make-up artistes) until the last minute. So you will need to make judgements based on previous experience as to the appropriate levels of make-up. This

make-up can be adapted or adjusted after the dress rehearsals or at whatever point all the elements are finally pulled together.

Whatever the size of stage it is vital that somebody from the make-up team pops out front several times during the final rehearsal to see the effect of each make-up from the audience viewpoint.

On tour

Productions that go on tour must plan for make-up that will work whatever the venue. It is unlikely that there will be time or opportunity to make any changes, unless these are very minor. The demands of the play and characters, rather than the venue, must dictate style.

Ballet and dance are inevitably a step into the world of fantasy. However modern the approach to the ballet or the dance sequence, the aim will be to create a visual world, one where it is the music, movement and expression that will carry the mood and narrative. This is a stylised world. Reality has been abandoned by the very choice of this medium.

In many instances, this gives the make-up artist a great freedom. Experimentation is the order of the day! New and exciting make-up can be explored.

Certain dance and ballet companies, however, may be very much bound by convention. And even when the company is keen to explore new ideas, particular productions within their programme may need to be conventional rather than experimental. Some

Make-up for ballet and dance

classical ballet productions, in particular, may need to conform to tradition.

It is vital that the make-up artist fully understands the company, the ethos of the particular production and the aims of the directors.

**Tips on creating
a classic ballet make-up**

For ballet or modern dance use a little more foundation than in a basic make-up, in a flattering colour. This may be quite pale but as with any character, much depends upon the role. A snow queen or swan will need a delicate pale colour scheme but if the character is an animal or bird – or a magician – then the role will make its own more colourful demands. The make-up suggested here is for a conventional classical dance role.

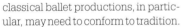

*Keep boys' make-up natural unless
the roles make specific demands*

Make sure all the make-up is applied carefully and well 'set' or powdered. Dancing roles can be energetic and the performer is likely to perspire.

Ensure a thorough application that is well finished to allow for this.

On white skins a soft, pale grey eye shadow will give a good effect without looking bright and over-coloured. Dancers with darker skins can look very good with a little lilac shadow.

To avoid eyeshadow being rubbed off, use a cream eye shadow. Then powder it well. On a large stage, add a little shimmer to enlarge the eyes.

For dancing roles, the eyes need extra emphasis. Draw a top eye line as well

Make-up for ballet and dance

as a bottom one with cake or liquid eyeliner. Choose a colour that matches the hair. Draw a fine line along the lash roots and extend it at the outer corner of the eye without letting it meet the top line. Mascara the lashes and define the eyebrows clearly.

The blusher position for dance should emphasise the cheekbones. Use the same colour as the previous make-up.

Very small girls should be made up with rouge in the natural position.

Lipstick should give clear definition to the lips, but use red or strong, bright pinks only on a really big stage. Red can look especially artificial and precocious on very young girls.

Boys will need careful make-up that is not extreme or obvious unless the role demands this. See the section on making up boys on page 71. In the same way, male ballet dancers should be made up in order to look appropriate under the lighting without being made to appear too feminine. (See pages 56-59 on making up men.)

Extravagant roles will demand extravagant make-up, of course, whatever the sex of the dancer. There are many ballet roles for men and women that can be really exciting to make up.

This is a world of fantasy that is often peopled with magical characters, animal roles and extremes of good and evil. All these roles can make great demands on the make-up team but will be very rewarding to undertake.

Fantasy and fairy-tale make-ups give the actor or dancer – and the make-up artist – great opportunities to be imaginative and to create something new and original.

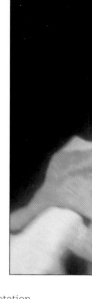

Non-realistic make-ups can vary from very theatrical exaggeration of normal human features to stylised representation of non-human forms. Animals, abstract paintings, mosaics, flowers and trees and so on – all come into this category.

The first thing to remember when creating this sort of make-up is that it must fit in with the production as a whole, so an overall guiding influence, such as the director or a make-up artist, is most important.

Another vital point to consider is whether the characters have become so familiar to the audience that any change in their appearance might be challenged. For example, the monster in Frankenstein will be forever the character as portrayed by Boris Karloff; and the Mad Hatter and all his friends in Wonderland will always be the characters illustrated so well by Tenniel. However, the three witches in Macbeth have no definitive portrait and so their appearance is always

open to a new interpretation.

It would be impossible to cover every character that an actor may be called on to create. Many of the make-ups explored in detail through step-by-step guidelines in this book will be applicable to a ballet or a fairy tale production – such as animals and witches. Here are just a few suggestions about fairy make-up to give some guidelines on how to approach this especially fascinating area of stage fantasy. It is hoped that they will 'whet the make-up artist's appetite' and open up the possibilities.

Fairies and elves

Fairies, elves and other kindred spirits can be good or evil. If they are evil, pointed noses and slanting evil eyes will suggest this.

In many ways, good fairies are more difficult since they really should look diminutive and ethereal. Good cast-

Pointed elf ears

Pointed elf ears can be made from latex but it is also possible to make them very effectively from adhesive plaster and hairpins.

1 Cut a strip of 50mm (2 inch) wide adhesive tape about 105mm (4.25 inch) long.

2 Place it sticky-side up and lay a fine hairpin on it, bent into an elfin ear shape.

3 Cut a circle of paper 37mm (1.5 inch) in diameter.

4 Fold it in half, and lay it along the bottom edge of your strip.

5 Fold the top half of the strip over the hairpin and the paper and press the two sticky surfaces together, trapping the hairpin and the paper between them.

6 Cut around the shape of the bent hairpin and along the bottom edge, to slice through the folded edge of the paper.

ing is the first essential and then the make-up needs to be especially delicate and precise.

Fairy foundations need to be very pale and pretty. Experiment with different shades; these can vary from the palest pink to pale blue, green or mauve. Sometimes designers suggest metallic gold or silver. However, a complete metallic face make-up can look very heavy and is more suitable for a robot. It is better to use a very pale base with gold or silver highlighting. A tiny tip-tilted nose looks very elfish or fairy-like and can be made with a small amount of nose putty.

Always check colours under the lights. Ballet, fairy tales and pantomimes may use a wide range of special lighting effects and these can change the make-up effects quite drastically. Check what is happening with lighting before planning the make-ups. The chart on page 19 explains some of the possible effects of the lighting.

7 Open out the end of the resulting ear shape. Cut away some of the tape and paper on one side in order to make the shape fit the front of the natural ear.

8 Colour the tape with greasepaint to match the skin colour and then stick it on to the natural ear – using spirit-gum.

9 These ears can be removed with spirit-gum solvent and reused several times if handled and stored with care.

Male and female impersonation

Men and women reverse roles in the theatre for a number of different reasons. Each of these reasons and each type of production will give rise to its own style of make-up.

Role reversal may be used for:

1
Glamorous female impersonation

2
Slapstick dames in English Christmas pantomimes

3
Principal boys in English Christmas pantomimes

4
Straight sex reversal in a Shakespearean production

5
Straight sex reversal in a Restoration production

6
Breeches parts in opera

Sex reversal may be used, of course, simply for the purpose of disguise.

Male and female impersonation

Female impersonation

Hopefully, the male performer playing a glamorous female impersonation role will have a suitable bone structure – one that is not too aggressively masculine. Then all that is necessary is to apply a glamour type of make-up. It may also be necessary to follow some of the principles laid down in the section on corrective make-ups (see pages 46-53).

Hints on achieving the right effect

1 Pay particular attention to the eyes, eyebrows and lips.

There is a huge difference between the outrageous dame character, who retains his masculinity, and the true female impersonation where the femininity can be utterly convincing

2 It is vital that you conceal the beardline. The actor should shave about half an hour before applying the make-up. Then, if the beardline is not too strong, it will be necessary only to add just a touch more foundation to the beard area. If the beardline is very dark, however, first stipple a covering film of cream-stick or grease foundation (approximately the same tone as the natural complexion colour) on to the beard area and thoroughly powder this to set it.

3 Then apply cake make-up over the entire face and throat, powder once more, and proceed with the rest of the make-up.

4 Check on the costume and how much flesh is revealed. At the very least the hands may need attention with a manicure and nail polish.

Male and female impersonation

5 Usually, a good wig is essential to complete this type of make-up but, if the actor's hair is sufficiently long, it can be dressed into a suitably feminine style.

Pantomime dames
The traditional dame of British pantomime needs a different approach since no attempt is made to conceal the fact that the part is played by a man. Every actor playing a dame tends to develop his own individual style of make-up, which can vary from simply putting on a wig and perhaps a lipsticked mouth, through to a complete make-up – similar to that used for over-made-up old women in Restoration comedy (see pages 131-132).

Male impersonation

Make-up for male impersonation varies enormously. There is the simple masquerade used in a Shakespearean production, when a woman dons a masculine costume, the hair is concealed beneath a hat or a man's wig, and the make-up is kept to a minimum. A boyish look is generally the intent for this 'pretty youth'.

Contrarily, a glamorous principal boy in pantomime may wear a man's costume but the make-up is essentially feminine and glamorous.

However, for full male impersonation where authenticity is the aim, very detailed make-up should be used, as described here:

1 Apply a dark foundation and stipple in beardline with medium-grey lining colour. Cover natural lip line with the foundation.

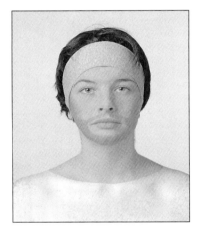

2 Highlight and shade the bone structure, paying special attention to the jawline, browbone and nose. Nose putty or a false nose can be used.

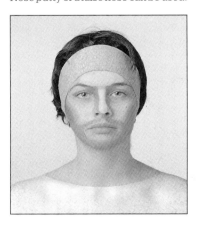

3 Lightly sketch in the eyebrows to give a fuller, more masculine shape. Then draw in the eyelines, blending away edges.

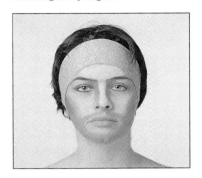

4 Add a false beard and moustache, if required, and put on a masculine-styled wig.

Musical productions

Musical productions

Musical productions tend to be fairly lavish affairs with a relatively large cast. The make-up will therefore need careful planning and organising. See also the section on *Group Make-up* on pages 35-36.

Each show will dictate its own needs but often there will be some quite exciting projects. This might be *My Fair Lady's* transformation of an actress first into flower-seller, Eliza Doolittle, and then a further dramatic change when she turns into the glamorous creation of Professor Higgins at Ascot and the Ball. Or it might be the exaggerated character make-up of Fagin in *Oliver Twist*; or the pierrot make-up required for *Oh, What a Lovely War*; or the 1920s flappers in *The Boyfriend*.

As with the ethnic make-up, it can be useful to collect images from theatre and film, as well as programmes and journals from a variety of productions of the musical that is planned – so as to create a dossier on the characters concerned.

Musical productions often have large casts. The make-up will need to be well organised and co-ordinated so that each individual becomes a part of the overall effect as here in a medieval musical revue (above), in Guys and Dolls *(centre) and in* Oh, What a Lovely War *(below)*

An overall coherent approach to all the make-up in a show must be decided upon well in advance, especially as a large cast means there is likely to be a team of make-up artists and/or individual actors doing their own make-ups.

Having decided on the approach to the make-up, that is, the overall style and then the individual make-ups, the head make-up artist will have sketched out make-up plans. Copies of these should be pinned up in the dressing rooms and it can be very helpful if each character has their own copy. This is especially important if

the actors are being 'processed' by a team rather than being allocated individual make-up artists.

Musicals, like children's shows and fairy tales, offer escapism and a chance to be really imaginative. Make the most of this opportunity by planning ahead well, researching all the possibilities and ensuring that you have sufficient team workers and a well-organised time structure in order to accomplish all that you plan.

Historical settings

When the play being produced is set in any other than contemporary times, it is vital to ensure that costumes, hairstyles and make-up are historically correct. There are many books that deal with this is great detail and make-up artists should find a good deal of reference material on 'faces through the ages' – so here are just a few brief notes on fashions in hair and make-up from some of the most popular historic periods depicted on the stage.

Egyptians: Cleopatra, *et al*

Shakespeare's
Anthony and Cleopatra
Shaw's
Caesar and Cleopatra

Egyptian tomb wall paintings show that civilised men and women used cosmetics extensively.

1
Eyes were heavily outlined with black galena.

2
Eyelids were coloured with green malachite.

3
The cheeks were rouged with powdered red earth or henna leaves crushed in cream.

4
Lips were coloured with carmine.

5
Skin was sometimes whitened with white lead for ceremonial purposes, but most Egyptians preferred their own sun-tanned complexions.

6
Eyebrows were shaved and new ones drawn on.

7
Men and women shaved their heads and wore elaborately styled wigs, or cut their hair into careful geometric tiers.

8
Most men were clean-shaven but patently false beards were worn for ceremonial purposes – even by Egyptian queens.

Ancient Greeks

Oedipus
The Rape of the Belt
Androcles and the Lion

Compared to the other ancient civilisations, the Greeks used cosmetics sparingly, so in the theatre the make-up is usually kept natural, particularly for men. Masks were worn for theatrical performances so these might be used for a contemporary play, or a very stylised make-up to reflect this powerful drama convention.

1
Women's make-up is pale with unrouged cheeks and muted lip make-up.

2
The eyes have the contour crease well defined, giving the lid a sculpted look.

3
Hairstyles were comparatively simple. Women piled their hair high on the top or back of the head and allowed spirals and ringlets to fall down their backs or loosely over the shoulders. Low foreheads were fashionable, so the hair was often dressed forward with curls.

4
Men generally kept the hair short, tightly curled, close to the head and, like the women, dressed forward over the forehead.

5
Most men had long and softly curled beards and moustaches.

Historical settings

Romans: Toga times

> *Julius Caesar*
> *Britannicus*
> *A Funny Thing Happened on the Way to the Forum*
> *Up Pompeii!*
> (plus characters in New Testament stories, such as Herod or Pontius Pilate)

For theatrical purposes, Roman make-ups need not be grossly exaggerated – except perhaps for more decadent characters. Appropriate costume and hairstyle will convey the instant impression of Ancient Rome. Of course if the performance is a comedy, then some exaggerations may then be acceptable.

1
Both men and women in Roman society whitened their skins.

2
They rouged their lips and cheeks.

3
Romans also dyed their hair and darkened their brows.

4
Women's hairstyles became more elaborate and complicated as the Roman Empire developed, with extensive use of false braids and curls piled on top of the head.

5
Men's hairstyles tended to be short, dressed close to the head, and combed forward over the forehead. Longer hair was bound with a fillet.

6
Most mature men were clean-shaven. Young men sometimes grew their beards until they attained their majority. Then they were ritualistically shaved and their beards were dedicated to the gods.

Medieval times and pantomime

> *Camelot*
> *The Lion in Winter*
> *Canterbury Tales*
> *Becket*
> *Robin Hood*
> *Dick Whittington*

Many pantomimes and fairy tales are set in the Middle Ages. Albeit the 'Dark Ages', it is often depicted as a very romantic time. In reality, men grew long, unkempt hair and beards. Cleanliness was not a priority and bathing became a thing of the past.

1
It was fashionable to be pale and often women were bled. They seldom added any colour to cheeks or eyes.

2
Women lightened their hair or (after marriage) hid it away beneath a veil or chin strap.

3
This exaggerated pallor was accentuated by plucking eyebrows and hairline, so that the face was smooth, white and without definition – like a large, white egg.

4
Unmarried women wore their hair long and flowing or woven into heavy long braids bound with ribbons. Sometimes they added false pieces so their hair fell well below the waist.

5
Later in this period, hair braids might be wound round the head, or coiled into elaborate chignons or pads over the ears.

Meanwhile, miracle plays required actors to make up with incredible realism and ingenuity as devils, saints, animals and angels.

Historical settings

Shakespeare and the rest

The Renaissance saw the opening up of new trade routes; make-up materials became more readily available. Indian red or Spanish rouge was used over a whitened skin but damaged the skin, so the make-up became even heavier to conceal this damage.

This is the time of Shakespeare's writing and a good number of his plays are contemporary.

1
During Henry VIII's reign, beards were generally very full and generously curled, but in the Elizabethan court they were trimmed into countless different shapes like the Spanish spade beard, the English square-cut, the forked beard the stiletto beard. Sometimes they were dyed red as a tribute to Queen Elizabeth.

2
Hair was brushed high up over wire frames and pads and then framed in crescent-shaped head-dresses, bejewelled with pearls and precious stones, or with tiny hats pinned to the summit.

3
By the end of Elizabeth's reign, wigs were fashionable – tightly curled or smooth and winged.

From the extravagant French court to the Puritans

The seventeenth century was a period of great contrast, ranging from the extravagances of Louis XIV's court to Puritan America.

1
The early century still saw high hairstyles and heavily painted faces for the women.

2
Men's hair was now worn longer and fell to the shoulders.

3
By the middle of the century, the beard had almost disappeared. Wigs became fashionable.

4
Women's hairstyles were built on wire supports to allow cascades of curls to stand well away from the face. Voluptuous 'peaches and cream' milkmaid looks became fashionable.

5
The Puritans arrived; the men with cropped hair and square-cut beards, the women looking pure and scrubbed, tucking all their hair into bonnets.

Historical settings

Restoration excesses; the French and American Revolutions and Georgian pomp

Tom Jones
She Stoops to Conquer
The Rivals
A Tale of Two Cities
The Scarlet Pimpernel
The Madness of George III
Cinderella
Amadeus

A time of great artificiality. Hairstyles rose higher and higher; wigs became ever longer and more voluminous.

The so-called Restoration make-up (which actually reached its peak in Georgian times, well past the restoration of Charles II) is looked at in more detail on pages 129-32.

It is important to analyse the approach to the play and its intrinsic style as well as historical authenticity. The Queen Victoria depicted here, like Cinderella, requires a more romantic make-up – not a realistic one

1
Women's hair became more and more extravagant, adorned with galleons in full sail, baskets of fruit and bouquets of flowers.

2
Men's wig styles were endless in their variety – bag wigs, bob wigs, club wigs, pigtail wigs, brigadier wigs, and scratch wigs (worn by working classes and now meaning cheap wigs used by melodrama comics).

3
Make-up was used extravagantly by men and women. Dangerous layers of white lead were used to whiten skins and caused many deaths.

4
Cheeks were over-rouged in circular or triangular patterns or just wild slashes of colour.

5
Brows were heavily blackened and eyelids brightly coloured.

6
Make-up for men reached its zenith in the 1770s, with elaborate powdered wigs, grotesque make-up and foppish dress.

Historical settings

From Napoleon and Josephine to Victoria and Albert

> Frankenstein
> Sense and Sensibility
> Murder of Maria Marten
> Oliver
> The Heiress
> The Woman in White
> A Month in the Country

Initially, as a reaction against the Restoration excesses, make-up was subtle – with short hair, carefully dressed. But fashion flows in waves: false hairpieces soon made their return. Napoleonic 'Jane Austen'

clothes gave way to early Victorian crinolines and late Victorian bustles!

For more details on Victorian melodrama make-up, see pages 132-34.

From Edwardian music hall and escapism to the First World War

> When We Are Married
> Gigi
> The Winslow Boy
> A Flea in Her Ear
> My Fair Lady
> The Seagull

Music Hall continued to be a very popular form of entertainment. Artifice started to reappear but the cosmetics used were now of a much higher standard.

Women

1
Topknots became fashionable in Regency times. Braids and chignons were pinned in place, and bejewelled bandeaus encircled the head.

2
Feathers, jewels and flowers were used in profusion.

3
During the Victorian era, cosmetics were not approved; obvious make-up was rarely seen.

4
Initially, hair was longer – braided and knotted close to the head. By the 1870s, however, more false hair was worn, with enormous chignons and falls of false curls.

6
Marcel waving meant the false piece disappeared. Softly waved hair was swept up over the ears to the crown of the head in voluminous topknots, dressed well forward to give a very high, full look to the front of the hair.

Men

7
In the early 19th century, men remained clean-shaven with short natural hair.

8
As the century advanced, facial hair became fashionable and, by the mid-century, beards and moustaches were almost universal.

9
Side whiskers dominated, with innumerable variations – 'mutton chops', 'Piccadilly weepers', long, flowing 'Dundrearies'. 'Burnsides', which crossed the cheek to join the moustache, were named after General Burnside in the American Civil War.

10
By the end of the century, beards had almost disappeared but moustaches remained.

Historical settings

1

The general effect was still very natural for younger women.

2

Older women, although looking made-up, did not seem garish in appearance.

3

Hair became fuller and wider, rather than higher, at the beginning of the period.

4

By the First World War, the full, heavy hair had gone. Worn wide, hair followed the natural shape of the head, lapping over the ears in soft coils.

5

Men were usually clean-shaven. Hair was of moderate length.

6

Older men occasionally sported a beard and moustache.

The Roaring Twenties

Hay Fever
The Boyfriend
Bugsy Malone
The Ghost Train
Juno and the Paycock

Make-up became obvious – and much more fun.

1

Eyebrows were plucked.

2

Mascara was generously applied to lashes.

3

Eyeshadow was popular.

4

Lips were strongly coloured and rosebud shaped.

5

Cheek rouge was no longer regarded as sinful.

6

Hair was bobbed or shingled. Fringes, bangs and curls were brilliantined on to the face and a tight bejewelled bandeau encircled the head.

7

Men sported pencil moustaches. Their hair was cut short and brilliantined close to the head or sometimes artificially waved.

30s and 40s: The Second World War and the impact of cinema

Cabaret
Night Must Fall
Cold Comfort Farm
Private Lives
The Dresser
Rebecca
The Prime of Miss Jean Brodie
The Long and the Short and the Tall

Make-up was now strongly influenced by Hollywood films. Despite restrictions imposed on the cosmetic industry during the war, women still

1

Make-up became more colourful and slightly theatrical in appearance.

2

Lips were larger and more sensuous, like those of Joan Crawford.

3

The brows were still plucked but, instead of being highly arched, they were now longer and curved softly downward, giving a languorous look to the face.

4

The mannish bob was gone: longer, softly-waved hair was all the rage. Hair was parted on the side or in the centre and gently finger-waved at the sides, ending in fluffy curls.

5

The snood, used to protect long hair in the munitions factories, became fashionable.

6

Moustaches became fuller in England, while in America they all but disappeared.

7

The war influence introduced men's short back and sides. The top of the hair was still waved, often being carefully dressed into place with finger and water waves.

Make-up for Restoration comedy

managed to imitate their favourite stars of the silver screen. Noel Coward was in full swing as were Fred Astaire and Ginger Rogers. Escapist musicals contrasted with the Depression and the war deprivations that followed.

After this brief historical tour, the make-up for Restoration plays and Victorian melodrama is now looked at in more detail.

Make-up for Restoration comedy

During the Restoration period, make-up was worn by both men and women from many different walks of life. The amount and style of make-up clearly denoted social standing.

Since there are a very large number of plays and operas which were written during or about this period and these are constantly being performed, it is very important to have a good understanding of the make-ups needed.

Young country girls and boys did not use make-up so these characters need no more than to look healthy and natural. Women in towns, on the other hand, from both the upper and lower classes, wore make-up and made no attempt to conceal the fact.

Key points in a Restoration make-up

1

Dark complexions were considered common so skins were whitened with rice powder, chalk or sinister washes made from white lead or zinc oxide.

2

Cheeks were heavily rouged. Ladies of delicacy and breeding used rosy pinks. Lower-class women tended to use strong ugly reds, as did older women struggling to retain their youth.

3

Eyebrows were darkened with carbon sticks. Coloured eyeshadow was used by the upper classes.

4

Wigs were used extensively, particularly by men who wore them over closely shaved heads. Styles varied from the very simple type worn by the working classes to the exaggerated extravagances of the Restoration fop.

5

Elegant men of fashion all wore flesh-coloured powder and a touch of rouge on cheeks and lips.

6

Patches were worn by both sexes, some for pure ornamentation, some to hide spots and pimples. Where they were placed on the face often had some significance, either sexual or political (Whigs patched to the right and the Tories patched to the left). Patches were made variously from velvet, silk or even black paper and were gummed to the face with mastic.

7

Many people during this period suffered from smallpox (then raging through Europe) or the disfiguring effects of venereal disease . . . so men often wore patches as well as heavy concoctions of lead and white zinc oxide to cover the scars. The more dandified they were, the heavier this make-up became.

Restoration fop

The Restoration fop must look as though he has spent a long time in front of a mirror meticulously caring for his appearance.

1 Any latex or putty noses should be applied now, before putting on the foundation.

2 Use a heavy application of a pale-pink cake foundation and stop the application short at the jawline – to give the face a mask-like look.

3 Arched eyebrows and an exaggeratedly tip-tilted nose add to the required effect. Block out the natural browline and boldly draw in the new eyebrows with black pencil or liner.

Sophisticated Restoration men and women

4 Eyelids can be shaded with coloured shadow, the eyes boldly outlined with black liner and mascara used heavily on the lashes.

5 Lips should always be obviously made up, with the shape suiting the character. For a soft effeminate look, use clear bright-red colours painted into a cupid's bow. For a more sardonic cruel character, the lips can be painted into a large sneering shape, using strong dark-red colours.

6 The cheeks should be strongly rouged with bright colours. Choose soft and pretty shades for the effeminate types – and strong scarlet for more evil characters.

7 Patches can be cut from black flocked paper and stuck on with spirit gum or simply drawn on with black eyebrow pencil.

8 Hands, neck and other exposed body areas can be left unmade-up in order to accentuate the over-made-up face.

9 A wig completes the foppish make-up.

Sophisticated Restoration women

Sophisticated women wore heavy and obvious make-up. Even if trying to make them more subdued and attractive, it is still important to retain the appearance of a very obvious make-up.

1 Apply a very pale pink-toned foundation, using either cream-stick or cake until an absolutely flawless finish has been achieved. If you are using cream-stick foundation, be sure to powder thoroughly.

2 Use a very pale or a white pigmented powder, rather than a translucent one, to give a porcelain finish to the make-up.

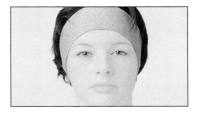

3 Delicately sketch in the brows, using very dark-brown or black eyebrow pencil. Keep the arch high and gracefully curved.

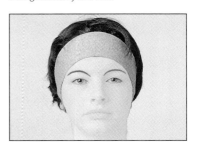

4 Highlight the top lid with white liner or cake make-up. If white liner is used, powder with white face powder. This highlight can be left white or very lightly coloured with a pale-blue or lilac powder shadow.

5 Now draw in the contour crease, keeping this high and with a well rounded shape.

6 Very finely outline the eyes. The line on the top lid should be kept very thin and as close to the roots of the lashes as possible. The lower line should be widest in the middle to give the eye a wide and round appearance. Apply mascara to both the top and the bottom lashes.

7 Paint on a generous and well-curved mouth, using bright clear reds or strong clear pinks, depending on the costume colour.

8 Brush on powder rouge to tone in with the lip shade, adding sufficient colour to achieve a good, strong rouged appearance.

9 Put on the wig and fasten it in place. Depending on the character, this can look like natural hair dressed in the period style or can be an elaborately dressed artificial wig in silver, grey or white.

10 Make up the hands and all exposed skin areas with cake or pigmented, liquid body-make-up, using a very pale colour so that the skin is almost white, with the merest hint of pink.

11 A small black patch (made of flock or drawn on with eyebrow pencil) may be used to complete the overall sophisticated appearance.

Over-made-up elderly women

One other very important character that is frequently met in Restoration drama is that of the ageing old harridan who uses every artifice to recapture her lost youth and looks.

If the actress is young, age the face very strongly and to make it as unattractive as possible.

If, the actress is already mature, exaggerate the highlights and shadows already present on the face and at the same time make it as ugly as possible.

Don't be afraid to overdo it. What may look overpainted and harsh in the mirror can frequently look quite pretty to the audience.

1 First, the ageing make-up should be executed with grease liners. Use very dark brown for the shadows and pure white for the highlights, which should be thoroughly powdered with translucent face powder.

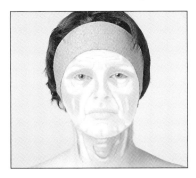

2 Apply the 'over-made-up look' over the top of this ageing make-up. First, with a fairly wet cosmetic sponge, apply a wash of a very pale, almost white, cake make-up. Stop the application short at the jawline so that the ageing make-up on the neck has maximum emphasis.

3 Draw on eyebrows with black pencil in one continuous hard line, arching them well up above the natural line of growth.

4 Apply a vivid splotch of very bright eyeshadow to the top lids.

5 Strongly outline the eye with black liner on a number 6 filbert brush. Extend the line on the top lid beyond the outer corner of the eye in a downward direction.

6 Make up both top and bottom lashes with a heavy application of black mascara.

7 Outline the mouth with black eyebrow pencil. Lift the centre of the exaggerated cupid's bow almost up to the nostrils and allow the ends to droop down at the corners of the mouth. The bottom lip should be well rounded but small. Fill in the lips with strong dark-red colour, using a number 6 filbert brush.

Victorian melodrama

8 With a rouge mop or a pad of cotton, very crudely apply the rouge to the centre of the cheeks, keeping the colour slightly low on the face.

9 Put on the wig, which can be very elaborately styled and made of obviously dyed hair.

10 Patches can be added, using black pencil or cut-outs from gummed flock paper.

11 Finally, the hands should be aged (see pages 68-69).

Victorian melodrama

Victorian melodrama is – like musicals, pantomimes and fairy tales – a grand excuse for some 'over the top' make-ups that are great fun to do. This was a period in drama when the villain was a gross exaggeration of evil and the heroine was pure innocence.

The villain

This character is an absolute theatrical 'standard'. He is the epitome of the smooth, dominant 'baddie' whom the audience love to boo and hiss.

Make-up detail will depend upon the age of the particular villain being portrayed but generally he will be depicted as middle-aged and relatively prosperous, even if his riches are ill-gotten. A swirling moustache and sleek appearance are essential.

1 After applying a base colour, age the character appropriately as described on page 63.

2 Sketch in strong eyebrows with black pencil. Start very low down by the top of the nose and wing the ends dramatically upward over the browbone to suggest a demonic trait.

3 Attach or create a strong moustache (see page 83). It must have suitable curling ends that the villain can twirl.

4 A scar can be an interesting addition. See pages 90-91 for details on how to make a convincing three-dimensional scar. Because this character is so 'over the top' and artificial, it may be an instance where drawing a scar on the face might just be acceptable but this must be done very carefully or the effect will simply look silly! Practise first. If there are a good number of performances then making a three-dimensional collodion scar that is reusable is probably more economical on time than drawing a new one every night.

Victorian melodrama

The heroine

This character must be sweet and pretty. She needs a beautiful rather than a glamorous make-up so that she looks attractive but not artificial. Innocence is the order of the day. Many heroines are poor girls whom the villain wishes to seduce so she should not be too sophisticated, either. The Victorian heroine might be a simple, healthy, country wench who is unaware of the villain's evil intents – or she might be depicted as a pale and delicate town girl, a fragile creature lost in a wicked world. These are two very different make-ups so far as colour range goes, with the county wench needing a healthy rosy complexion and the city waif a pretty pallor, but in both cases, a round-eyed innocence must be stressed.

Victorian 'tart'

This lady must be lively, obvious and over made-up, Whether or not she is a character with whom the audience sympathise depends upon the play but bear this in mind in her treatment.

1 Use a very pale foundation, like an ivory, to give the skin suitable pallor. Finish this make-up at the jaw line so the artificiality is emphasised.

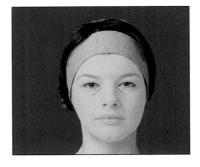

2 Use shading to create tiredness shadows.

3 If required, build up lines and highlights from the nose to the mouth (see ageing make-up on page 62).

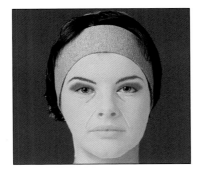

4 Highlight the shadows. The fashion was for faces to be less angular, rounder then than now so, unless the actress is plump, do not shade and highlight for structure.

5 Powder heavily: use a pale, loose powder.

6 Draw black eyebrows in a thin line or heavily darken the natural shape. Greasepaint, artists' pencils or black boot polish were used in Victorian times to achieve this end. Black cake eyeliner is a good substitute today.

7 Heavy, bright eye shadow gives a suitably cheap, eye effect. Take this shadow right over the lids and close up to the eyebrows. The Victorians used greasepaint so cream or stick eyeshadow gives a more authentic look than powder eyeshadow but it will need a little gentle powdering over to keep it from smearing into the eye creases.

8 Draw a heavy black line around the eyes with a pencil or, for a smudged look, a grease liner will work very well.

9 Mascara is optional but make it natural looking. The Victorians did not use mascara.

10 A little white eye shadow under the eyebrows adds to the artificial look.

Victorian melodrama

11 Prostitutes rouged their faces heavily with theatrical make-up. Use bright pink or scarlet blusher – or lipstick. Make a round, doll-like shape in the centre of the cheeks.

12 Lips were rouged with grease-paint in very basic garish colours. Use the brightest red possible to draw a rounded, bow-shaped lip line. Smudge this if you feel it is appropriate for the character.

13 Check how the make-up looks from a distance.

14 If appropriate, you can dirty the face, neck and hands with grease or cake eyeliner.

15 A beauty spot can suggest an inept attempt at elegance.

16 Untidy the hair and perhaps tie it back – or up – with cheap, shiny ribbons.

17 A bruise or a black eye might complete the rough effect of the character.

18 Nicotine tooth enamel will dirty the teeth, or one can be blacked out entirely – but do not attempt this on capped teeth.

Whether Restoration, a fairy-tale pantomime or an historical play, special shows will provide the opportunity for some very creative and imaginative make-up. Although demanding, these plays will be great fun for both the make-up artists and the actors

Exciting characters

Fantasy and magic

While the large part of the make-up team's time will be spent on the creation of relatively straight make-ups, every now and then productions arise where there is the opportunity to do the more exotic 'escapist' make-ups.

Children's productions, fairy tales and pantomime, cabaret and revues, plus plays with a magic or animal theme are most likely to involve extravagant make-ups but of course there are witches and ghosts of various kinds in Shakespeare plays while some plays with a conventional cast may involve the odd rather more dramatic character make-ups.

For instance there is the ghost conjured up in Noel Coward's *Blithe Spirit* or the Frankenstein lookalike in the comedy thriller *Arsenic and Old Lace*, while, plays like *Jekyll and Hyde*, *Count Dracula* or *The Wind in the Willows* will all obviously involve a good deal of 'special effect' make-up.

In many ways, because of the element of escapism, these make-ups are not only great fun to do but can often – however time-consuming – be easier than, say, an ageing make-up where realism is essential. None the less, as ever, do check on the ethos of the play and overall production approach to ensure the make-ups are treated appropriately. A 'send-up' or 'over the top' make-up would be out of place in

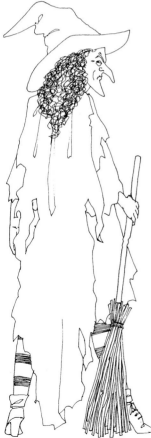

Traditional witches have hooked noses

Traditional witches have the following ghastly features:

A large, hooked nose

A sharp, pointed chin

Sunken cheek hollows

Tiny, deep-set, evil eyes

Heavily wrinkled skin

Hairy warts

Tight, thin lips concealing almost toothless gums

Long, straggly hair

Claw-like hands with long, curved, dirty fingernails

Dark, dingy complexions with sallow-yellow or green undertones

Hags are much the same but may be plumper with bulbous rather than hooked noses.

a serious play or might not be in keeping if the humour depends upon a 'straight' approach.

Hopefully you will be able to enjoy creating a whole range of fantasy make-up creations during your theatre career. Meanwhile here are a few ideas to inspire experimentation.

Witches and wizards

Witches can be good or bad; they can be beautiful or ugly – but the make-up described here is for the conventional evil, ugly witch so often required in the theatre. Note: Before you begin the make-up, apply false noses and chins, using nose putty or prosthetic pieces. Long noses and pointed chins are easily knocked, so the prosthetic type is definitely preferable.

Witches and wizards

1 Apply foundation colour. Use the grease or cream sticks, with a stippling technique to give a broken appearance. A green make-up can work well.

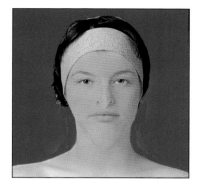

2 Shade and highlight the face very strongly. Use black or very dark olive-brown for shadows, and white or yellow for highlights.

3 Sketch on very heavy, severe eyebrows with a black pencil, – or use false brows.

4 Intensify the eyes with black liner.

5 Add red liner to the inside edge of the lower eyelids.

6 Attach warts with spirit gum or latex adhesive.

7 Add strands of dark-grey crepe hair to the chin with spirit gum.

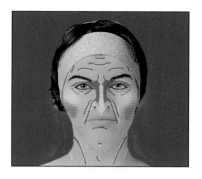

8 Draw in a thin, mean mouth with black eyebrow pencil.

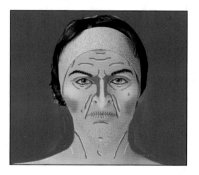

9 Blacken the teeth with tooth enamel. (Check that they are not crowned or capped first.)

10 Fasten the wig in place. Alternatively, use raffia, grey wool or teased-out sisal string – dyed a suitable colour and sewn around the edge of the witch's hat or hood.

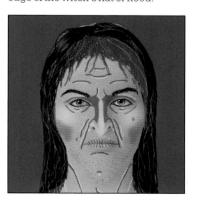

11 Bony knuckles look effective. Paint the knuckles with spirit gum, allow it to dry slightly and add a small ball of cotton (cotton wool) to each knuckle. Cover the cotton ball with a coat of sealer and allow it to dry.

12 Then make up the hands. Use an exaggerated version of ageing make-up. Highlight and shade the false knuckles to make them as bony as possible (see pages 68-69).

13 Long witches' fingernails can be added, using heavy acetate or old photographic film (see page 95). Paint the nails with black, grey or green nail enamel.

Note: If time is short, a simpler way of dealing with the hands is to wear ragged dirty mittens, leaving just the fingertips and nails to be made up.

Wizards

Wizards, like witches, may be evil or benign. The make-up must be adapted accordingly, but the essential for any wizard make-up is to intimate eccentricity, wisdom and magic.

Demons and devils

Demons and devils

The archetypal devil, such as Mephistopheles, has the following:

A long, thin face

Sharp, pointed features

A long nose

Narrow, well-defined lips

Black eyebrows: these are close together, curving dramatically upwards

Dark, deep-set eyes that wing in the same direction as the eyebrows

A thin moustache

A small, pointed goatee beard

He may have horns

1 Block out the ends of the eyebrows to allow the browline to be winged up.

2 Use a very pale foundation with green undertones.

3 Paint in highlights and shadows very strongly to emphasise bone structure with strongly angled cheekbone shading. Use dark olive-brown or black for shading and white or ivory for highlights.

4 Sketch on the eyebrows with a black pencil. Start very low down by the top of the nose and wing the ends dramatically upward over the browbone.

5 Outline the eyes with black liner. Start well in at the inner corner, close to the nose, and wing the outer corner up towards the browbone, parallel with the brows.

6 Mascara the lashes.

7 Add red liner to the inside edge of the lower lid.

8 Outline the mouth with black pencil. Keep top lip long and thin. Fill in the lip shape with very dark lake liner. Darken the top lip with the pencil.

9 Add a beard and moustache.

Demons and devils

10 Put on and fasten the wig.

11 If using the natural hair, draw in the 'widow's peak' with an eyebrow pencil.

12 Make up the hands to tone in with the face. Accentuate the bone structure with strong shading to make the hands look as thin and long as possible.

This devilish make-up can be adapted to create other characters such as Dracula, Richard III, Iago from *Othello* or the Demon King in pantomime. Suitable adjustments will be necessary. For Iago in *Othello*, for example, you should make the foundation dark and swarthy.

For Dracula and other vampires

1
The arched brow line, as used for the Devil, is ideal.

2
Dracula will need fangs.

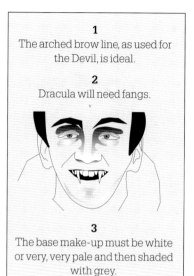

3
The base make-up must be white or very, very pale and then shaded with grey.

4
Dracula is always clean-shaven so do not add a beard or moustache.

5
Vampire fangs: Bones from the butcher or a taxidermist can be used for fangs but they will need to be boiled and bleached before being pierced into a strip of foam rubber and then glued into place there. They will then be ready to be worn in the mouth or sewn onto a costume or a mask.

For the Demon King

This is yet another version of the devil make-up but with the following changes and additions:

1
The foundation can be red.

2
A red sequin stuck to the centre of each eyelid will give a fiery flash as it catches the light.

3
Sparkle might be added to highlight the cheekbones.

Check if the demon king will be appearing under coloured lighting as this will change make-up colours so they may need to be adapted accordingly (see page 19).

Death and ghosts

Death

Generally, the character of Death wears an all-enveloping black cloak and hood, with just the skull and hands visible. Basically he must be an ominous figure, portending death to those unfortunates who see him.

Features

Skull head – or faceless

Pointing skeletal hand

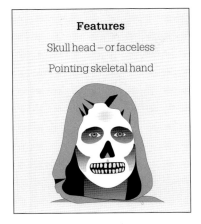

1 First block out the eyebrows completely with cream stick.

2 Next apply a heavy, pale ivory foundation over the entire face. Stop at the jawline.

3 Shade the temple and cheek hollows deeply, with dark-grey liner.

4 Draw in the eye sockets in a sloping-down pattern.

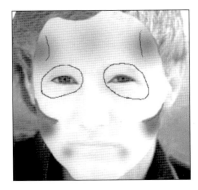

5 Lightly shade the depressions in the centre of the forehead and just below the lower lip on either side of the chin.

6 Intensify the temple and cheek hollows with black liner.

7 A skull needs to have black eyes. Completely blacken in the top of the eye socket.

8 Draw in the nostril openings. Start just below the bridge of the nose and make a triangular shape over the sides of the nose. Blacken the inside of the nostrils but leave a hairline of pale foundation down the centre of the nostril flange.

9 Use black eyebrow pencil to draw in the teeth along the top and bottom lips. Extend them out at the corners of the mouth until immediately below the end of the eye.

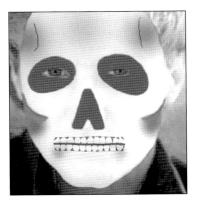

10 A skeleton needs leering teeth. To emphasise this effect, you can blacken the centre of the mouth with a line of black pencil. Extend this out at the corners of the mouth, between the two sets of teeth.

11 Apply black foundation over the neck. This should meet the ivory face colour in a sharp line along the jawbone.

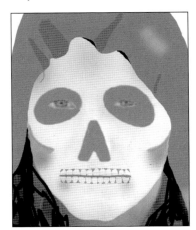

12 Make up the skeletal hands.

Monsters

Ghost

A ghost can most simply be achieved with an eerie mask but it is far greater fun to experiment with ghost make-up – and may be essential if the ghost has to speak many lines.

> A skeletal face might be appropriate, with hollow eyes.
>
> White or translucent make-up will work well.
>
> Add a pinky red outline around the eyes and nostrils.
>
> White out the lips and add grey lines to suggest skeletal teeth.

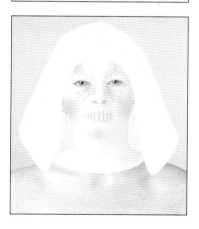

Monsters

The approach to a monster make-up depends upon the style of the production. If the production is an adult horror play, then the monster should be as realistic and frightening as possible; a more sympathetic approach should be used for children's entertainment; while a humorous or 'over-the-top' make-up would work in a comic production.

The monster might be a distorted human being or have animal characteristics. Or it might be an alien with relatively few recognisable conventional features! (See also *Aliens* on page 142.) The script should be looked at closely before deciding on an appropriate make-up.

Creating a monster is quite a challenge and may need the combined forces of the wardrobe, properties, special effects and the make-up teams. Much depends on whether the head is to be the actor's own or a mask. Explore all the possibilities. These roles are all figments of the imagination, the stuff of fantasy, dreams and nightmare, so it is a wonderful opportunity to escape the normal bounds and to experiment.

Good monster details

> #### Many special 'monster' effects can be used, such as:
>
> Nose plugs to flatten and coarsen the nose
>
> Open wounds with streaming blood
>
> Distorted or extra eyes – or perhaps just one false eye
>
> Appropriate scars and wounds
>
> Horns or antennae
>
> Wild wigs
>
> Extreme facial colouring
>
> Lots of hair or shaggy fur
>
> Scales on the face and hands
>
> Tentacles on the head
>
> Claws on the hands
>
> Fangs and horns

Remember that warts and blemishes can be made of rice-crispies or pieces of odd-shaped macaroni.

Wrinkles and folds of flesh can be made from cheesecloth soaked in size, shellac or PVA (white flexible glue) and then squeezed into shape.

Crinkled flesh might be suggested by spaghetti, softened in hot water, shaped while pliable and then left to dry out again into interesting shapes which are then stuck onto the skin with spirit gum.

Useful tips
Rummage through joke shops for a fascinating choice of fingers, noses, claws and teeth.

A monster head can be made from a strong paper sack. This should be pasted over with several layers of newspaper and paste and then painted with emulsion paint (latex).

Lightly boiled eggs can be scooped out and painted to make strange, staring eyes. Paint them first with a mix of PVA glue and white paint to make them rigid and then add the final detailing. Half ping-pong balls might also be used.

Dragons

A dragon will need the following:

Strong colouring, usually green

Scales

Huge teeth or fangs

A fire-breathing tongue

Reptilian eyelids

Once again this is where good research and lots of illustrative reference will inspire the most effective make-ups.

Werewolves

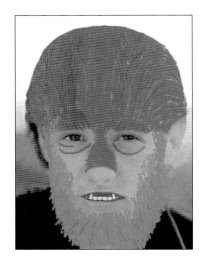

A good wig will be an essential element of this make-up. Werewolf wigs can be made to resemble animal hair growing low on the forehead or with hair which appears to grow from the browbone and then covers the entire face with an abundance of facial hair.

Once the right wig has been organised, the addition of fang-like teeth and coarse flattened noses, can be very effective.

Teeth for Dracula and monster make-ups are best made by a dental technician so that they fit comfortably in the actor's mouth. However, this can prove a very expensive exercise and will not be in the budget for a short run.

If the actor does not have to speak a great deal, quite effective teeth can be made by embedding animal teeth (which can usually be purchased from taxidermists) into a thin strip of foam rubber, using a strong glue. This strip is then pushed up under the top lip, in front of the gums. If this does not appeal, false teeth from a make-up shop might be used instead but do ensure a relatively comfortable and secure fit (see also *Vampire fangs* on page 138).

Main features

Shaggy hairy wig

Wolf or dog like features, especially the canine muzzle

Lots of facial hair, very low down the forehead or sprouting from brow bone

Dog teeth

Medusa

Medusa, the Gorgon, has a head of snakes instead of hair. In the original Greek legend these snakes writhe about and turn men to stone.

Plastic toy snakes or electrical flex can be attached to a buckram wig base, a short-haired wig or a bathing cap.

If your stage structure allows, or if the scenery can be organised to accommodate this, some of the snakes can be played like a marionette and made

to wriggle by attaching invisible threads and taking these to a suitable vantage point above or to the side of the monster. Accompanied by loud hissing sounds, these moving serpents could look very effective.

A strange eerie face colour will help the overall effect.

Frankenstein's monster

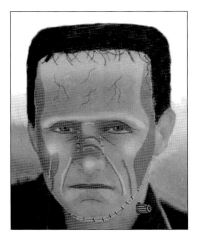

Frankenstein's monster will need:

A high, square-topped forehead

Heavy eyebrows

Bolts through the neck

Scars

This well-known monster needs a good wig with a built-up forehead. This should be made to fit right over the eyebrows to give the classic hairless browbone effect. The monster's heavy false eyelids can be made from adhesive plaster.

Since the flesh should appear to be 'stitched together', long cuts can be

Aliens and robots

applied with Derma Wax. The stitching can be simulated by using staples or small pieces of a fine hairpin bent into shape and pressed into the wax.

Neck bolts can be made by taking the caps off old electric-light bulbs and sticking them to rubber washers which provide a suitable surface that can be stuck to the neck with spirit gum.

Aliens and robots

Aliens

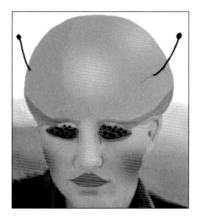

An alien is really just another living life form and can assume almost any characteristics – human, animal, insect-like or whatever the particular play dictates.

Anything goes, including:
Antennae
Extra heads or other facial features such as ears
Pointed elfin ears
Strange skin colour
Distorted humanoid features
Metallic skin texture or scales

To make antennae, use one of the following:
Pipe cleaners threaded through egg boxes
Tightly twisted aluminium foil
Washing-up bottle tops
Toilet roll tubes
Dowelling
Bed springs
Plastic piping
Microphones
Toothbrushes
Felt
Wire
Tentacles
Cable or cord
Suction caps from children's toys
Plastic corrugated vent pipe

To make eyes, try
Ping pong balls
Fimo
Clay
Foil
Marbles
Buttons
Bottle tops
Foam balls
Painted egg shells

For fangs and teeth, try:
Foam
Polymer clay (such as Fimo)
Strong cardboard
Pieces of plastic cut from food containers (such as yoghurt tubs)

For hair and beards, use:
String or cord
Wool
Wood shavings
Ric-rac braid
Raffia
Fake fur
Paper
Feather boas
Dry macaroni stuck on a base
Crepe hair from a make-up supplier
Christmas garlands (dark green is good)
Reels of old photographic film
Crepe paper slashed and rolled

Robots

While the creation of a robot is likely to be largely the wardrobe department's responsibility, if the robot is to talk and respond, it will be much easier for the actor if the face can be seen. In this case the make-up department will need to be involved.

To achieve the appropriate mechanical effect, gather in everyday household items like egg cartons,

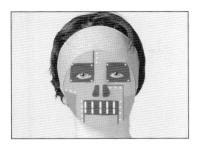

Some ideas . . .

Bed springs can be used instead of ears.

An old motor-cycle helmet can be a good base for a robot head.

Papier mâché can be layered inside saucers to make small satellite receivers.

Wire or sized string can be wound around tubing to give a turning or cork-screw effect.

Wire antennae can be topped by a ping pong ball. Hooks off the top of shower gel bottles can also look effective at the top of the antennae.

A metallic foundation such as silver, or gold or copper will work best. Mixed with a green, blue or purple, they can be even more effective.

Sparkle can also be added to the make-up.

Shiny, metallic wigs, combined with a metallic make-up, can work very well for a humanised robot.

Painting squares and oblongs like metal plates, onto the face gives a good mechanical effect. Gold or silver 'rivets' can be added along the metal seams.

yoghurt pots and toilet-roll tubes. Once they have been sprayed with metallic paint they can make useful additions to a make-up or wig.

Animals

Make-up for animal characters can be approached in two ways: realistically or non-realistically. For the realistic approach, a fur-covered latex mask or headpiece needs to be made by a model maker with the eyes and mouth then made up to blend in. This approach is best for such roles as the lion in *Androcles and the Lion* or for the cat in *Dick Whittington*, which are non-speaking characters.

The make-up department should have in their portfolio a collection of animal images. It is good to have a mix of natural photographs and cartoon images. The first is very useful refer-

ence, especially when the more realistic make-ups are needed. The cartoons are sometimes even more helpful as the artists will have already defined the obvious features of each animal; this will help the make-up artist to clarify the most important elements in a make-up, too.

Clearly, extra reference material can be collected together once the cast requirements are fully understood. Sometimes the animal characters are not actually named and may be a motley collection of woodland creatures, pets or whatever. In any case, the more reference material available, the better equipped you will be.

Humanised animals like Toad and Badger in *Toad of Toad Hall* need a stylised face make-up that blends in with a suitable head-dress or hat. The actor's own hair might be dressed in a suitable style.

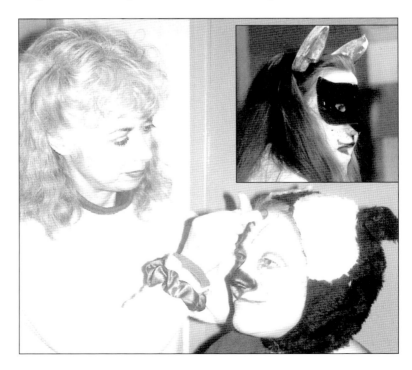

Animals

Toad

1 Block out brows with Derma Wax to create prominent browbones.

2 Apply a yellow foundation.

3 Draw on heavy lids with black pencil and white highlight.

4 Add pouches under the eyes.

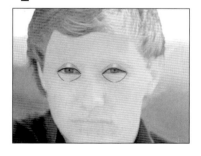

5 Draw in high eyebrows with a black pencil.

6 Darken the inside of the nostrils

7 Draw on a toad's mouth with lake liner and black pencil. Highlight the top lip with white liner.

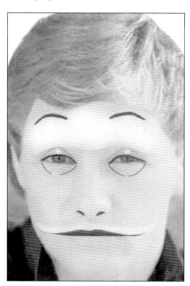

8 Dress the hair down well with solidified brilliantine and make a centre parting or side parting, to flatten the top of the hair. Or you can use a wig and dress this.

Badger

1 First apply a very pale or white foundation.

2 Shade the face with dark grey or brownish black to create a striped badger pattern. Outline the eyes with black liner.

3 Add a beard, moustache and false eyebrows.

4 Dress the hair with hair whitener in a striped badger effect. Brush the hair up as much as possible before spraying with lacquer. Wigs in the right style and colours are hard to find, but a very dark brown wig, sprayed with silver, may be an alternative to dressing the actor's own hair.

5 Do not make up the mouth.

Lion

1 Disguise the eyebrows – especially if they are dark and bushy. Use spirit-gum for this but no wax, as the raised hairs can be teased into the fur effect later.

2 Apply foundation. Cake foundation is good for animal make-ups. Ensure the colour suits the mane and costume but if in doubt, a dark olive tan works very well for lions!

3 Assuming this is a male lion, a full moustache and a small beard should be glued into place. If the beard shape needs any adjusting, first spray this with gel, and then pin it up to set appropriately.

4 Trace in the eye shape and the lion nose with a dark brown eyebrow pencil. Make sure that you cover the end of the actor's own nose.

5 Use creamy cake make-up to draw on the right fur effect. Sketch in the main dark brown areas, being sure to include a distinct 'V' shape on the forehead.

6 Paint on a white fur effect around the eyes and on the beard and moustache.

7 Draw fine white strokes up over the eyebrows and then onto the forehead.

8 Draw in a strong cat's-eye shape with black.

9 Cover the entire eyelid with very dark shadow, rising to a point in the centre.

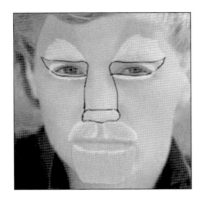

10 Colour in the end of the nose. Take the black colour around the nostrils. Draw a strong black straight line down to the moustache.

11 Curve the black line away on both sides into a suitable cat smile effect.

12 Dot and stipple black onto the white area of the moustache.

13 Darken the lower part of the beard but retain the rounded shape of the white area.

14 Slightly darken the lower lip with a little grey-brown mix.

15 Add shading colour to the forehead. Next use this shading colour to create high cheekbones and then to suggest folds down the sides of the lion's muzzle.

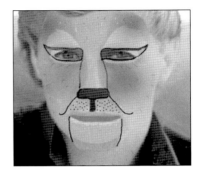

16 Now darken the sides of the moustache.

17 Use black to outline the edge of the white beard.

18 Add dark brown strokes as needed – probably onto the cheeks, under the eyes and down the visible area of the neck.

19 Soften the 'V' on the forehead with strokes and stipples of white and brown.

20 Fix on the lion wig and dress this as needed to create the right shaggy, lion-mane effect.

Animals

If there are several lion roles (or whatever animal) try to vary the make-up details to distinguish the characters from each other

For tigers

Use:

1
A yellow-orange foundation

2
Black stripes

3
Strong whisker markings

4
A black nose and white muzzle stippled with black dots

5
Elongated eye make-up to give an appropriate slanted-eye effect

Cats, dogs, rabbits, mice, pigs and so on

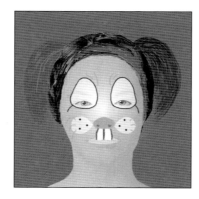

As ever, how much detail can be undertaken depends on the amount of time available and whether this is a fast change or not. Also, while some animal costumes are detailed and definitive, others are rather amorphous 'cat-suits' and depend greatly on the face make-up and the ear shape to convey the right message as to the particular animal intended.

Even these details can be misinterpreted if the rest of the make-up is just flat colour. It is a combination of all the elements that matters. Big floppy ears could intimate either a spaniel or a lop-eared rabbit! Large long teeth, either sketched in above the mouth or worn as three-dimensional teeth will instantly convey rabbit but then again it might be a mouse. In this instance, the right-shaped ears will differentiate between the two.

So to achieve the most convincing animal make-up, analyse the following:

Face shape and colour

Face texture (for example, is the face spotty, or wrinkled?)

Nose shape and colour

Mouth shape and colour

Whisker shape and size

Eye shape (are the eyes rounded, long, slanted, large, small, button-like, or whatever?)

Once the research has been done, keep notes like this in your portfolio for future reference.

Birds

Clowns

The make-up necessary for birds can be analysed in the same way as animals – based upon a good collection of information. In particular, check out beak shapes and colours as these will dominate the make-up. Obviously the costume colours and feathers will convey a strong message but getting the make-up right is still vital. For example, the make-up for an owl's eyes would be very different to the make-up needed for a parrot.

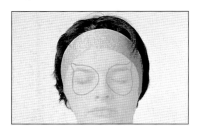

Owl

1 Apply a suitable overall golden brown base.

2 Using a darker chocolate brown, draw an oval shape all around each eye, with an uplifted 'flick' at the end so that it looks rather like a very rounded quote mark.

3 Fill in most of this shape with the chocolate brown colour but leave a circle free immediately around the actual eye.

4 Fill in the circle around the eye with a golden brown colour.

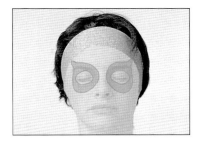

5 Draw in a black outline around this central eye colouring.

6 Apply white streaks that radiate out over the chocolate brown areas surrounding the eyes.

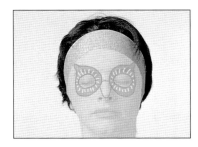

7 Create a beak outline on the nose with black pencil.

8 Fill this beak shape with yellow or orange and then add a sharp, black central line down the beak.

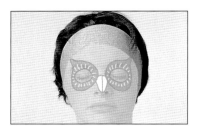

9 Add some soft, feathering effects around the edges of the face with the lightest brown or with white.

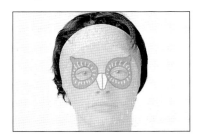

Clowns

Traditional clown make-up falls into two distinct groups: white-faced clowns and tramp clowns. Both of these groups can be further sub-divided into sad and happy clowns. Sad clowns have mouths and eye make-ups that slant downwards, and happy clowns have wide-awake eyes and upturned mouths.

Wigs are worn by both white-faced and tramp clowns and can be as silly as you wish.

147

Clowns

Examples of white-faced tramp and clowns

White-faced clowns

White-faced clowns are usually paint-ed with 'clown white', a special, very opaque grease make-up which is easy to apply and provides a really good cover.

Other white foundations can be used, however, if clown white is not avail-able. Try the following method of whitening the face:

1 Apply a thin film of white grease or cream-stick make-up evenly over the face.

2 Thoroughly powder with white face powder.

3 Add a wash of white cake make-up over the top. This prevents the base colour cracking and so revealing the natural skin tone below.

4 No shading is used. Cheek colour is usually drawn on in clear geo-metrical shapes that are outlined with black pencil.

5 Heavily overpaint or block out the natural browline.

6 Draw on a completely new brow-line shape. These might be large half circles, inverted 'V's, sinuous curves and even flashes of lighting. The brows may even be completely asymmetrical.

7 Make up the eyes dramatically. These might have tears, vertical 'blips' or dots on top and bottom lids. Alternatively they might be outlined in black with an upward to downward slant. It all depends on the chosen clown character.

8 A single wash in a very bright colour can be used for eyeshadow.

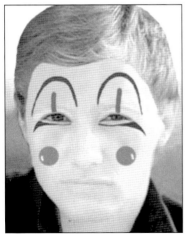

9 Mouths can be wide or small, neat and well defined. They should be executed in clear red with an outline of black pencil.

Tramp clowns

For tramp clowns, the make-up is usually very comic. Generally they have the following:

1
A strongly coloured foundation.

2
Huge over-painted mouths in red or white with the corners turning strongly up or down.

3
The mouth is surrounded by an obviously painted-on beard line.

4
The eyebrows are generally very high and in the shape of an inverted 'U'. This 'U' is often infilled with white or a very bright clear colour.

5
The eyes might be shaped like stars, triangles, or complete circles – or any appropriate shape.

6
Most tramp clowns have big, red, bulbous noses. These may be bought ready-made from joke shops. Alternatively, the end of the nose can simply be painted bright red.

Toys

Toys can be humanised creatures like dolls, soft toys like animals, or inanimate objects like trains and tops.

Pirates and Gypsies

Dolls

A doll-like make-up can be achieved as follows:

1 Use very pale pink or creamy-white foundation. Apply this foundation quite heavily to give a porcelain finish to the skin.

2 Add pink rouge in a distinct round spot to the centre of each cheek. Blend the edges very softly.

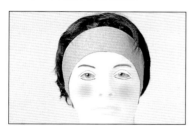

3 Draw on nicely rounded eye-brows, blocking out the natural brows if necessary.

4 Eyes should look as round as possible. With a black eyebrow pencil, draw a line in the crease at the back of the top lid. Make this as round a shape as possible.

5 Draw a circular line under the lower lashes and then fill inside this circular pattern with some white cake make-up.

6 Complete the doll eyes by adding very pointed, long, false lashes.

7 Paint the mouth in a small, exaggerated cupid-bow shape.

8 An inexpensive wig made of nylon, with braids or a mass of curls, will complete the doll effect.

Teddy bears and other soft toys

Most soft toys, including teddy bears, will be very closely related to animal make-up, but must be endearing.

Teddy bears should have the following make-up features:

1
A small black round nose.

2
A smiling mouth, drawn in a similar way as in the lion's mouth make-up on page 145, but with clearly defined, smiling ends!

3
Like dolls, teddy bears need round, bead-like eyes.

4
Whiskers are optional.

Toy soldiers

These should be made up with red, circular cheeks on a pale base and black, shiny flattened-down hair.

Pirates and Gypsies

In both cases, the characters might be male or female, dashing and attractive or rather threatening, so do some careful character analysis before planning the make-up in detail. If, for example, the gypsy is a mysterious fortune teller or a dancer entertaining

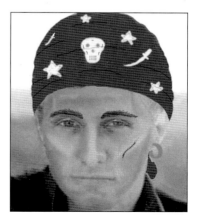

by the camp fire, then her make-up would be rather more exotic and flattering than say, that suitable for an old gypsy selling pegs.

In the same way, a pirate like Long John Silver will need far more exaggerated character make-up than would be used for a handsome, hero-type pirate. However, whichever type of characterisation is needed, this make-up will always be fun to do and will present interesting challenges. Whatever their age or sex, pirates and gypsies are usually romantic, exciting stage characters whether in *The Pirates of Penzance* or *Carmen*.

These are usually strong characters and will need similar make-ups in the following ways

1

A good, tanned foundation is needed, with a swarthy Mediterranean look (see pages 113-15).

2

Strong bushy eyebrows are useful.

3

Beauty spots and scars might add interest.

4

Use only the minimum of powder so that a suitable greasy look is retained.

5

Headscarves are generally 'de rigeur' so it is easy to conceal the natural hair, if necessary. False pieces or wigs might then be worn.

6

Big, round, brass ear-rings complete the effect.

Statues

To obtain a bronze effect:

It is probably best to use one of the proprietary bronze skin sprays but follow the instructions very carefully.

You can also make your own mixture, using bronzing powder, glycerine, water and alcohol. Apply a thin coat of this mix to all the exposed parts of the actor's body.

In either case, however, the skin pores can become clogged up with this kind of make-up so the bronze effect should never be done too far in advance or left on for long periods.

To obtain a coloured effect:

Liquid make-up is available in a variety of colours such as blue, red, green and purple. Always follow the instructions carefully with any of these 'special effect' make-ups.

To obtain a marble effect:

1 Apply white cake make-up to cover all the exposed skin.

2 Create the marbling effect with gold liquid make-up applied in a streaked effect over the whitened area.

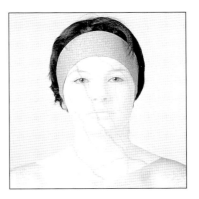

3 Give skin a sheen by gently polishing it with the palms of the hands or silk chiffon.

To sum up

This section on exciting make-up contains just a few examples of the multitude of special make-ups that are waiting to be explored by an enthusiastic make-up artist.

Hopefully, the ideas suggested will be useful and will inspire greater experimentation with stage make-up. Make-up is a highly creative part of theatre and as such, can be particularly rewarding. To begin with a straight face and turn it into something completely different is an exciting experience – for the make-up artist and the actor alike.

Useful addresses

UK

F16 Make-up
Mail Order

Tel: 01223·561795
E-mail:
sales@f16.co.uk

*Supplies a great range of
cosmetic and stage
make-up, from some of
the world's leading
companies, including
Kryolan, Leichner, and
Dermacolor*

Faces Of Distinction
Withybow Farmhouse
Withy Grove
Highbridge
Somerset
TA9 3NP

Tel: 01278 795225
Fax: 01278 793111
E-mail:
sales@face-paints.com

*Face painting & cosmetic
products by mail-order*

Charles H Fox Ltd
22 Tavistock Street
Covent Garden
London
WC2E 7PY

Tel: 020 7240 3111

The Make-up Centre
The Old Church
52a Walham Grove
London
SW6 1QR

Tel: 020 7381 0213
Fax: 020 7381 0213
E-mail:
info@themake-
upcentre.co.uk

Screenface
24 Powis Terrace
London
WC2 9LL

Tel: 020 7221 8289

Stage Lighting
Services
11 Gedling Road
Carlton
Nottingham
NG4 3EX

Tel: 0115 961 9988
Fax: 0115 956 1966

Zeller International
Unit 1C Brunel Way,
Mart Road,
Industrial Estate,
Minehead,
Somerset,
TA24 5BJ,
UK

Tel: 01643-707-659
Fax: 01643-706-492
E-mail:
snaz659@aol.com

USA

Abracadabra
10 Christopher St
New York, NY 10014

Tel: 212 627-5745

19 West 21st St.
New York, NY 10014

Tel: 212 627-5194
Fax: 212 627-5876

*Rentals, Indian costumes,
headdresses, necklaces,
spears, peace pipes. 6ft
cigar store Indian. Magic
tricks, gags & novelties,
make-up, masks, wigs,
magician supplies*

ADM Tronics
Unlimited, Inc.
224-S Pegasus Ave
Northvale, NJ 07647

Tel: 201 767-6040
Fax: 201 784-0260
E-mail:
admt@sales.com

Make-up adhesives

Alcone Company, Inc.
(Paramount Theatrical
Supplies)
(Mail Order)
5-49 49th Ave.
Long Island City, NY 11101

Tel: 718 361-8373

(Retail store)
235 West 19th St.
New York, NY 10011

Tel: 212 633-0551

*Theatrical make-up,
stage blood, theatrical
supply house in LIC.
Make-up cases, brushes,
supplies. NY store has
limited quantities for
make-up artists*

Benefex Inc.
Tel: 212 228-93C7

Special effects make-up

Bob Kelly Wig
Creations
151 West 46th St.
9th Floor
New York, NY 10036

Tel: 212 819-0030

*Custom made wigs,
theatrical make-up &
cosmetics*

Frank Bee Costumes
Center
Tel: 718 823-9792

*Rentals, Halloween &
mascot costumes, make-
up & wigs, magic
supplies*

Halloween Adventure
104 Fourth Avenue
New York, NY 10010

Tel: 212 673-4546

*Rentals. Huge collection
of costumes, swords,
masks, hats, wigs, etc.*

Kryolan Corporation
132 Ninth Street
San Francisco,
CA 94103

Tel: 415 863-9684
Fax: 415 863-9059

Mainstage: North
129 W. Pittsburgh Avenue
Pensacola, FL 32505

Tel: 414 278-0878
Fax: 414 278-0986
E-mail:
mts-north@mainstage.com

Mainstage: South
2515 W. Cervantes St.
Milwaukee, WI 53204

Tel: 850 434-2080
Fax: 850 434-6046
E-mail:
mts-north@mainstage.com

Make Up Mania
Tel: 800 711-7182
Fax: 914 426-1515
E-mail:
makeupmania.com

*Cosmetics, FX makeup,
ethnic wigs & make-up,
custom wigs & facial hair,
professional supplies.
Overnight delivery*

Make-Up Center
155 West 55th St.
New York, NY 10019

Tel: 212 977-9494
Fax: 212 977-9497

*Make-up & supplies,
stage blood*

Manhattan Wardrobe
Supplies
245 West 29th Street
10th Floor
New York, NY 10001

Tel: 212 268-9993
E-mail:
mwsupply@aol.com
Web:
www.wardrobesupplies.
com

*Stage blood, ageing and
distressing supplies*

Useful addresses

Mehron Inc.
100 Red School House Rd
Chestnut Ridge, NY 10977

Tel: 845-426-1700
Tel: 800 332-9955
Fax: 845-426-1515
E-mail:
info@mehron.com

*Theatrical make-up
and kits*

The Makeup Shop
131 West 21st St.
New York, NY 10011

Tel: 212 807-0447
Web:
www.themakeupshop.com

*Make-up supplies for
film, TV & print artists.
Tattoos, bald caps, latex
pieces.*

**Playbill Cosmetics /
Ideal Wig Co.**
Tel: 718 361-8601

*Wholesale. Make-up in
pencil form*

Ray Beauty Supply
721 Eighth Ave.
New York, NY 10036

Tel: 212 757-0175
Fax: 212 459-8918

*Rentals. Beauty salon
supplies, some
equipment*

**Seinazur Ademain
Cosmetics**
15 West 28th St.
5th Floor
New York, NY 10001

Tel: 212 779-9094
Fax: 212 779-9160
E-mail:
lee1818@ix.netcom.com

*International
manufacturer of
professional make-up
brushes, make-up and
kit products*

Alan Stuart Inc.
49 West 38th St.
New York, NY 10018

Tel: 212 719-5511
Fax: 212 719-5267

*Wholesale make-up, hair
brushes and combs*

Temptu Marketing
26 West 17th St.
New York, NY 10011

Tel: 212 675-4000
Fax: 212 975-4075

*Make-up, stage blood,
tattoos*

Uriel Bendrihem
E-mail:
urielb@inter.net.il
Web:
www.bendrihem.co.il

*Hand made professional
make-up cases. Made in
Spain from mahogany,
oak, cherry & maple
woods*

Zak's Fun House
2214 86th St.
Brooklyn, NY

Tel: 718 373-4092

Wigs, masks

**Zauder Brothers/
M. Stein Theatrical
Cosmetics**
10 Henry St.
Freeport, NY 11520

Tel: 516 379-2600

*Full line of make-up,
cream, greasepaint,
custom wigs*

Zeller International
Main Street Box Z
Downsville, NY 13753

Tel: 800 722-USFX

also at
1214 Metro Park Blvd.
Suite 201
Lewisville, TX 75057

Tel: 972 221-8665
Fax: 972 221-8625
E-mail:
snazaroo@mindspring.com

Further reading

Gill Davies
Create Your Own Stage Effects
A & C Black (UK) 1999
Watson-Guptill
(USA)1999

Gill Davies
Create Your Own Stage Production
A & C Black UK 2000
Watson-Guptill USA2000

Reggie Wells and Theresa Foy Digeronimo
Face Painting : African-American Beauty Techniques from an Emmy Award-Winning Makeup Artist
Henry Holt & Company (USA) 1998; 2000

Sherrill Leathem
Fantastic Fun Face Painting
Sterling Publishing (USA) 1997

Rosemarie Swinfield
Hair and Wigs for the Stage
A & C Black (UK) 1999

Thomas Morawetz
Making Faces, Playing God: Identity and the Art of Transformational Makeup
University of Texas Press 2001
ISBN:0292752466
Hardcover
ISBN:0292752474
Paperback

Kathryn A Quinlan
Makeup Artist (Careers without college)
Capstone Press (USA)1999
ISBN:0736801758

Lee Baygan
Makeup for Theatre, Film and Television
Drama Book Publishers

Anthony Timpone
Men, Makeup and Monsters: Hollywood's Masters of Illusion
St Martins Press (USA) 1996
ISBN:0312146787

Margaret Lincoln and Rob Shone
Most Excellent Book of Face Painting, the
Copper Beech Books
Library Binding - 1997

Rosemarie Swinfield
Period Make-Up for the Stage: Step-By-Step 1997
ISBN:155870468X

Juliao Sarmento, et al
Racial Makeup
Korinsha Press 1998

Richard Cummings
Simple Makeup for Young Actors
Plays, Incorporated 1990

Richard Corson and James Glavan)
Stage Makeup
Allyn & Bacon 2000/2001
ISBN:0136061532

Laura Thudium
Stage Makeup: The Actor's Complete Step-By-Step Guide to Today's Techniques and Materials
Backstage Books (USA) 1999
ISBN:0823088391

Rosemarie Swinfield
Stage Makeup Step-By-Step : The Complete Guide to Basic Makeup, Planning and Designing Makeup, Adding and Reducing Age, Ethnic Makeup, Special Effects
Betterway Publications 1995

Gill Davies
Staging a Pantomime
A & C Black (UK) 1995

Jim Roberts
Strutters Complete Guide to Clown Makeup
Players Press and Java Publishing Co, (US) plus Picadilly Books 1991

Sidney Jackson Jowers, John Cavanagh (Editor)
Theatrical Costume, Masks, Make-up and Wigs
Routledge, an imprint of Taylor & Francis Books Ltd 2000

J. Michael Gillette
Theatrical Design and Production : An Introduction to Scene Design and Construction, Lighting, Sound, Costume, and Makeup
Mayfield Pub Co 1999

Glossary and UK/USA terms

Accent rouge
rouge used to highlight the high point of the cheekbone

Acetone
clear liquid, harsh for the skin but used to dissolve collodion (scar material) and sealer

Alcohol
isopropyl alcohol (99% strength) is used to dissolve spirit gum and clean brushes and gummed laces on ready-made beards, moustaches, and wigs

Antimony
brittle, bluish-white, metallic substance

Bald cap
cap to cover hair for bald make-ups

Beard black
used for one to two days' beard growth, applied with a stipple sponge

Beard block
a wooden block in the shape of a face, used for laying on beards with latex

Beard stubble
waxy material available in small, flat containers

Blender front
wig with a gauze 'forehead' – good for creating receding hairlines

Blood capsules
can be filled with cherry or chocolate syrup for internal bleeding.

Brilliantine
a hair cosmetic which imparts a gloss

Cake make-up
greaseless, water soluble foundation

Carmine
crimson dye derived from cochineal, which is in turn derived from a Mexican beetle

Ceruse
a white paint derived from lead

Chignon
large coil of hair created at the back of the head

Chinese eyelids
made of latex, used for creating oriental eyes

Cloth mâché
fabric (usually cheesecloth) and glue mix that can be moulded

Clown white
opaque, white face paint, which gives strong coverage

Cold cream
for removing make-up and smoothing out waxwork

Collodion
colourless, gummy liquid which dries very quickly and so is useful for creating scars

Composite colours
different coloured sheets of lighting gel cut and then fitted together into one colour frame

Cotton buds
cotton swabs

Cotton wool
British term for cotton balls or cotton

Crepe hair
Crepe wool is the familiar braided wool often refered to as crepe hair. Crepe hair originally comes straight, and is then passed through a special machine to make it 'crepey'

Derma Wax
trade name for a pliable material that is used for making cosmetic builds

Dowelling
wooden headless pin

Dummy
baby's pacifier

Emulsion paint
water-based household paint available in the UK and called latex paint in the US

Fall
period hair piece, used only if you have long hair to match its length

Filbert brushes
brushes which are broad at the base but taper to a fine point

Fillet
headband for binding the hair

Fimo (polymer clay)
material that can be moulded and then baked to set, generally sold at craft stores

Fishskin
very strong, fine animal tissue

Foundation
base colour application upon which rest of make-up is built

Fuller's earth
a white-to-brown natural substance, which resembles potters' clay when mixed with water

Galena
common lead ore

Gel
gelatinous jelly-like substance

Gelatines (gels)
coloured filters which can be placed in front of a light

Glycerin
sticky sweet liquid, used for tears and perspiration

Hairlace
net foundation for making wigs and beards

Hard-edge wig
wig with hair knotted into place right up to its front edge

Hue
variety or tint of a particular colour

Key
a base, which will aid adhesion

Kohl
powder or pencil to darken eyelids, often made from antimony

Latex
adhesive, originally the fluid from the rubber plant, or material for artificial pieces made from this

Latex pieces
ready-made false pieces include latex scars, moles, bruises, wounds, chins, noses, eyebags, wrinkled foreheads, blind eyes, etc.

Lining colours
colours in a fine form that can be used for adding detail

Liquid latex
used to make small latex pieces; used alone on the face to create ageing

Malachite
green colouring derived from hydrous carbonate of copper

Marcel waving
hair-waving method named after a Parisian hairdresser

Masque
black colouring, similar to mascara, used to darken the hair and scalp

Mastic
natural resin from tree bark

Music hall
revue with old-time Victorian or Edwardian theme

Nasolabial
between the base of the nose and the mouth

Nose putty
special material for building or reshaping noses or other features

Orange stick
wood stick used to press down artificial eyelashes, to create a cut in a wax scar, or as a modeling tool

Orbital
the overall area of the eye socket

Pacifier
baby's dummy

Glossary and UK/USA terms

Pantomine dame
a comic matronly character, usually played by a male comedian

Papier mâché
paper pulp and glue mix that can be moulded

Pate
top or crown of the head

Physiognomy
the art of judging character from the features of the face

Pigment
colouring matter or dye

Plaster of Paris
quick-setting material used for making casts and moulds

Plastic adhesive
used instead of spirit gum for prosthetic pieces and bald caps in film and television

Powder, translucent
this particular powder does not change the color of make-up

Primary
main or first

PVA
white flexible glue

Rheumy
watery, as of eyes, but also nose and mouth

Sealer
clear liquid, used as a protection over wax or clay noses and chins; it dissolves in acetone

Scar material
non-flexible collodion used to simulate deep cuts in the skin or scars

Shading rouge
rouge which is used to hollow the cheeks

Smile pad
the raised cheek area, which is formed on the face by a smile

Spirit gum
liquid adhesive, good for artificial beards and moustaches

Subcutaneous
beneath the surface of the skin

Switch
length of artificial hair

Teat
nipple of a dummy (pacifier)

Translucent powder
semi-transparent powder that will fix make-up without altering its colours

Wings
area to either side of the acting area

Wool crepe
braids of inexpensive artificial hair for creating false beards and moustaches

Reference files

Make-up artists, and those actors who regularly do their own make-up, will find it very useful to build up a reference file of information on various aspects of characters and style.

Indexed correspondence files might be useful for this purpose – and can be used to store both written and visual information. The latter will probably be most valuable.

You will need to cross-reference clearly but material might be compiled under the following headings:

History of faces
Famous faces
Portraits from history

Accessories:
Spectacles
Ear-rings,
Hair ornaments . . .
and so on

Animal faces
Real animals
Make-up examples of animals

Present-day faces
Faces from different nations
Famous contemporary faces
(such as the British Royal Family, politicians, cinema and television stars)

Related subjects
History of hairstyles
Wigs
Modern beards and moustaches
Historical beards and moustaches

Fantasy faces:
Goblins and elves
Monsters, Witches
Robots
Aliens
Fairies

The ageing process
Children
Young faces
Middle-aged faces
Old faces

Interesting facial features:
Noses
Ears
Mouths
Scars
Wounds

Interesting make-ups achieved in previous productions

Make-up checklist

Boxes with dividers will be required to contain the following:

	In stock	Must reorder/buy	Received
Brushes			
A face-powder brush			
3mm (0.125 inch) flat			
6mm (0.25 inch) flat			
9mm (0.375 inch) flat			
Number 2 filbert			
Number 6 filbert			
Rouge mop			
Black tooth enamel			
Clown white			
Cotton (wool) balls			
Cotton buds (swabs)			
Derma Wax			
Eye shadow			
Eyebrow pencils			
Eyeliners			
False eyelashes			
False fingernails			
False noses			
Foundations			
Hair bands, grips and pins			
Hairpieces			
Latex			
Lining colours			
Lipsticks			
Make-up remover			
Mascara			
Moustaches or wool crepe			
Nose putty			
Powder puffs			
Robes			
Rouge			
Scissors			
Skin tonic			
Sparkle in gel			
Spirit gum			
Stage blood			
Tissues			
Towels			
Translucent face powder			
Wigs			

Index

Index

Index

Acknowledgements

The author wishes to thank Cowbridge Amateur Dramatic Society,
Minchinhampton Players and, in particular,
Avening Players for so many photographs – and so much fun!

Thanks are also due to the editors at A & C Black and
Back Stage Books of Watson-Guptill Publications for all their very
helpful advice and guidance.